Museums Along the Arroyo
A History and Guide

MUSEUMS
Along the Arroyo

A History and Guide

BY JANE APOSTOL

THE HISTORICAL SOCIETY OF SOUTHERN CALIFORNIA
Los Angeles, California
1996

Copyright, 1996
HISTORICAL SOCIETY OF SOUTHERN CALIFORNIA

LIBRARY OF CONGRESS CARD CATALOG NUMBER 95-82227
ISBN 0-914421-17-4

Produced under the direction of
THE ARTHUR H. CLARK COMPANY
Spokane, Washington

Contents

Foreword   9

Acknowledgments   11

Los Angeles in the Sunny Seventies and Booming Eighties   13

Heritage Square Museum   27

El Alisal: The Lummis Home   47

The Southwest Museum   67

Along the Arroyo Seco   81

Pasadena Historical Museum   103

The Gamble House   115

Museum Information   131

Selected Reading List   133

Index   137

Illustrations

LOS ANGELES IN THE SUNNY SEVENTIES AND BOOMING EIGHTIES

Los Angeles in 1876   13
Pico House in 1875   14
1880 lithograph of Perry Residence   16
Steamer *Ancon*   18
Cover of *Semi-Tropical California*   20
Charles Fletcher Lummis in 1885   22
Real estate advertisement   24

HERITAGE SQUARE

Entrance to Hale House   27
Palms Depot   28
William H. Perry Residence   30
Hale House   32
Valley Knudsen Garden Residence   34
Stable and carriage barn   36
Longfellow-Hastings Octagon House   38
John J. Ford House   40
Lincoln Avenue Methodist Church   42
Proposed layout of drugstore interior   44

EL ALISAL

Entrance to El Alisal   47
El Alisal under construction   48
The *museo*, or exhibit hall   50
Sketch in Lummis's House Book   52
"The Lion's Den"   54
El Alisal dining room   56
Mad Hares invitation   58
Lummis as carpenter   60
Wildflowers at El Alisal, 1905   62
El Alisal in 1986   64

MUSEUMS ALONG THE ARROYO

SOUTHWEST MUSEUM
Tunnel entrance to the Southwest Museum   67
Making a wax-cylinder recording   68
The Southwest Museum around 1920   70
"Apache Spirit"   72
George Wharton James with baskets   74
Hopi pottery maker   76
Fiesta at Casa de Adobe   78

ALONG THE ARROYO SECO
Crest of the Arroyo Guild   81
The Arroyo Seco after a flood   82
USC's College of Fine Arts   84
Cover of *Arroyo Craftsman*   86
Olive Percival in her garden   88
Abbey San Encino   90
Ernest Batchelder House   92
Jean Mannheim studio   94
Fireplace in the Hindry Residence   96
La Miniatura   98
Early scene in the Arroyo Seco   100

PASADENA HISTORICAL MUSEUM
Entrance to the Fenyes Mansion   103
Hotel Green dining room, 1896   104
Fenyes family members   106
Studio of the Fenyes Mansion   108
Tom Mix on the Fenyes estate   110
Finnish Folk Art Museum   112

THE GAMBLE HOUSE
Entrance to the Gamble House   115
The Gamble House under construction   116
The Gamble House entry hall   118
The living room   120
The dining room   122
Rear patio of the Gamble House   124
Front view of the house   126
Charles and Henry Greene in 1908   128

Foreword

Los Angeles in the 1870s and 1880s promoted itself as a place where wealth could be acquired and enjoyed. Brochures hawked climate, health, longevity and economic opportunity. Stately Victorian homes were built and real estate was quickly bought and sold. New communities grew like gourds in the night. Los Angeles was focused on the future.

Into this hustling business town in 1885 walked Charles Lummis. As author, editor, photographer, and librarian, he would become a forceful, enterprising advocate of preserving the past. For this purpose he founded the first museum in Los Angeles, the Southwest Museum, which opened to the public in 1914. Since then, Los Angeles museums have greatly increased in number and have made their influence felt on the cultural scene.

In this book Jane Apostol tells the story of five museums which are located within six miles of each other. Although individually Heritage Square Museum, the Lummis Home (El Alisal), Southwest Museum, Pasadena Historical Museum (Fenyes Mansion) and the Gamble House offer a distinctive slice of this region's history, collectively they build upon the rich legacy of the Arroyo Culture. In sum, as the author shows, they complement each other in remarkable ways. *Museums Along the Arroyo* is their story.

Jane Apostol, prize-winning historian and prolific author, is uniquely qualified for this assignment. With clarity and skill she presents each museum's history, explores the interconnections between them, and places each within the context of the history of Los Angeles, Pasadena and the Arroyo. Her language moves effortlessly in an unadorned graceful style. There is no straining after effect. She has mastered the ease of conversation in writing history. In scholarship and style, Jane Apostol has produced another benchmark in local history.

Museums Along the Arroyo is both timely and instructive. It arrives as museums across the nation are emerging as the modern-day keepers of our culture. As an informative guide it will introduce the people of Los Angeles and Southern California to the experience of five museums easily visited on a weekend. As history it shows how the past was lived, preserved, and is now promoted at the local level. In the process it calls attention to the importance of collective memory—a shared past that is the basis for personal and social identity and pride.

As the public appetite for museums grows (one hundred million now visit museums and historic sites annually in the United States), museums must develop new ways to work together to reach the public. Six years ago one person, Barry Herlihy of Heritage Square Museum, began that process for the Arroyo. The result today: five institutions working collectively as the "Museums of the Arroyo" (MOTA). The publication of their story in this book—and in an accompanying video—is the result of his interest, involvement and support.

THOMAS F. ANDREWS
Executive Director
The Historical Society of
Southern California

Acknowledgments

It has been a pleasure to write about the Museums of the Arroyo, whose varied holdings and public programs enrich the visitor's appreciation of art, architecture, history, and ethnology. I extend warm thanks to the following museum representatives for their generous help:

Thomas F. Andrews, executive director of the Historical Society of Southern California (which has headquarters in the Lummis Home); and staff members Margaret Dickerson, Carole Dougherty, and Michael Sanborn;

Jane Auerbach, executive director of the Pasadena Historical Museum; Judi Hunter, the former director; Tania Rizzo, archivist; and Linda Weber, museum educator;

Edward R. Bosley, executive director of the Gamble House; Randell L. Makinson, director emeritus; and Greene and Greene Library volunteers Doris Gertmenian, Louise Mills and Nancy Parsons;

Barry Herlihy, executive director of Heritage Square Museum; and staff members Karin Burd, Stephen Nelson, and Christine Donegan Springhorn;

Duane H. King, executive director of the Southwest Museum; Kim Walters, director of the library; and Barbara Arvi, curator of education.

I extend thanks also to Brita Mack and Jennifer Watts, curators of historic photographs at the Huntington

Library; and to Sue Mossman, executive director of Pasadena Heritage.

I also appreciate the help of Mary Borgerding, Sarah Duncan, and Millie Kirsch, volunteers in the Research Center of the Pasadena Historical Museum; and the help of Pat Copley, on the volunteer staff of the Southwest Museum.

In addition I thank Sally Beck, David Cameron, Jayne Kistner, and Virginia Neely for sharing their knowledge of local history.

Special thanks go to Thomas F. Andrews, who suggested a book on museums along the Arroyo and who coordinated the myriad details involved in its publication. The Historical Society of Southern California, which published the book, is pleased to acknowledge Associated Foundations Incorporated for supporting the project with a generous grant.

In conclusion, a loving thank-you to Tom Apostol, my favorite editorial consultant.

JANE APOSTOL

Facing page: Los Angeles as photographed by Carleton Watkins in 1876. *Courtesy of Huntington Library.*

Los Angeles in the Sunny Seventies and Booming Eighties

"'El Pueblo' came of age between dawn and dusk of the 5th day of September, in the year of our Lord, 1876," wrote Phil Townsend Hanna in his lively introduction to *Los Angeles in the Sunny Seventies–A Flower From the Golden Land*. It was on September 5, 1876, that Charles F. Crocker, president of the Southern Pacific Railroad, hammered a golden spike into the final section of track giving Los Angeles an all-rail connection with San Francisco and the East Coast. "The most auspicious event recorded in the annals of our city," proclaimed the editor of the *Los Angeles Daily Star*. Los Angeles was on the way to becoming a great metropolis.

In 1876 adobes were disappearing from the city, and homes and businesses were moving south of the Plaza area–for a century the residential, social, and commercial

The Pico House, acclaimed in 1870 as the finest hotel south of San Francisco. *Courtesy of Huntington Library.*

center of Los Angeles. Extensive orchards and vineyards still were planted within the city limits, and "semi-tropical" nurseries downtown advertised orange, lemon, lime, and walnut trees for sale. Los Angeles had eight newspapers, including one in Spanish, one in French, and one in German. The city boasted a self-styled opera house, a theater, and a public library with a collection of two thousand books.

Despite the opinion of one early cleric that Los Angeles was more a city of demons than of angels, by 1876 the moral climate had so improved that there were a dozen houses of worship. Among them was the first permanent church in the city (Our Lady of the Angels, dedicated in 1822), the first synagogue (Temple B'nai B'rith, dedicated in 1873), and the first cathedral (St. Vibiana's, dedicated in 1876). Both the synagogue and the cathedral were designed by Ezra F. Kysor, who also designed the three-story Pico House, a splendid hotel that opened for business in 1870. The symbol of a changing era, it was built on a site long occupied by the adobe mansion of Don José Antonio Carrillo. "Progress and improvement have this week laid their relentless hands upon one of the old and very familiar landmarks of the city," lamented the *Los Angeles Star* when the adobe was razed.

The Pico House (erected by former governor Pío Pico) and Our Lady of the Angels (where mass is still celebrated) are among the significant buildings preserved in their original setting, in what now is designated as El Pueblo de Los Angeles State Historic Monument, which is located in the Plaza area–the birthplace of the city. Other historic buildings in the 42-acre park include the city's first firehouse, its first theater building, and one of its first brick buildings.

A splendid residence built in 1876. *Courtesy of Huntington Library.*

LOS ANGELES IN THE '70S AND '80S

A number of other historic structures, threatened by demolition, have been moved from their original sites in Los Angeles and Pasadena and relocated in Heritage Square Museum, on a strip of land paralleling the Pasadena Freeway and the Arroyo Seco. (Dry for most of the year, as its name implies, the Arroyo Seco is a watercourse extending from the San Gabriel Mountains to the Los Angeles River.) The W. H. Perry House, which now can be seen in Heritage Square, once occupied a view lot in the garden suburb of Boyle Heights. Ludwig Salvator, Archduke of Austria, visited Los Angeles and the Perry House in 1876. He published his thoughtful observations on the city in *Eine Blume aus dem Goldenen Lande oder Los Angeles*, later translated as *Los Angeles in the Sunny Seventies*. The decade was not altogether sunny, however. In 1871 a mob attacked residents of the Chinese quarter, killing nineteen people. In 1875 Los Angeles suffered from a devastating drought, a smallpox epidemic, and the failure of one of its three banks. Nevertheless, said one jaunty observer, Angelenos emerged from the slough of despond to pull off the greatest demonstration the town had ever seen. This was a grand Fourth of July celebration in 1876 honoring the hundredth anniversary of the Declaration of Independence. "There was more than the usual amount of powder burned, some whisky (but no blood) spilt," wrote a contemporary historian, "and everybody was sublimely happy, and noisily patriotic." A featured event of the celebration was the issuance, on July 4, 1876, of *An Historical Sketch of Los Angeles County, California* (often called The Centennial Sketch). Written by three distinguished residents–J. J. Warner, J. P. Widney, and Benjamin Hayes–the booklet is noteworthy as the first published history of the city and county.

The steamer *Ancon*, which connected San Francisco and San Pedro before completion of a rail link in 1876. *Courtesy of Mary Helen Wayne.*

LOS ANGELES IN THE '70S AND '80S

"Los Angeles is about twelve miles from the coast, and one has to make about as many flank movements to reach it as Sherman made to reach Charleston," wrote Jennie Collier, who traveled from San Francisco to Los Angeles in 1876 before the rail link was completed. After a six-day train trip from Keokuk, Iowa, she boarded a steamer in San Francisco, reached San Pedro two days later, transferred to a tug for the three-mile journey to Wilmington, and from there went by train to Los Angeles, twenty-five miles away. Although admitting that the city was the most prosperous in Southern California, she was not enchanted by its "conglomerate smells and picturesque filth."

Jennie Collier--with her sister, Margaret Collier Graham, and Mrs. Graham's husband–had left the Midwest to make their home in California. Like many other new settlers, they had read a persuasive 1872 bestseller, *California: For Health, Pleasure, and Residence. A Book for Travellers and Settlers,* by New York editor and author Charles Nordhoff. It sold some three million copies, was translated into Spanish, French, and German, and is credited with doing more than any other book or article to attract settlers and travelers to California. Nordhoff praised the landscape, the productiveness of the land, and the benefits of the Southern California climate for consumptives and other invalids. He wrote in some detail about growing citrus, olives, walnuts, and almonds in Southern California and described "the brilliant pecuniary returns" yielded by groves and orchards.

Another book with enormous influence on emigration was published in 1874 by Major Ben Truman. The title of the book--*Semi-Tropical California: Its Climate, Healthfulness, Productiveness, and Scenery*—sums up its exuberant con-

A noted example of booster literature.
Courtesy of Huntington Library.

tents. "After reading Major Truman's glowing account of Semi-Tropical California," wrote a San Francisco reviewer, "it requires some self-control to prevent one from rushing off incontinently to the Southern Coast and forswearing San Francisco forever."

Booster literature helped bring thousands of prospective settlers to Los Angeles. Between 1870 and 1880 the city's population nearly doubled, going from 5,728 to 11,183. "The demand for residences and business houses is unprecedented," said the *Herald Pamphlet of 1876*. "In Los Angeles a house is generally rented before the plans are in the hands of the contractor." Colonel Robert Baker helped supply the need for residential and commercial space by putting up an enormous building at Main and Arcadia Streets in 1878. The three-story Baker Block had arcaded entrances, two large cupolas, and a tower rising 110 feet above the mansard roof. The building displaced El Palacio, the elegant adobe home of Don Abel Stearns, who died in 1871. Don Abel's widow, Arcadia Bandini de Stearns, married Colonel Baker, and the couple maintained a fashionable apartment on the third floor of the new Baker Block. A number of attorneys had offices in the Baker Block; and among the ground-floor tenants were a dry goods store, a liquor store, a seed store, and a Japanese art store.

Los Angeles celebrated the city's centennial in 1881. The following year it celebrated proof of its modernity. The Nadeau Hotel became the first four-story building in town. The telephone company extended service to its first ninety subscribers, among them the new University of Southern California. And on New Year's Eve 1882 the first arc lamps (mounted on 150-foot poles) lighted downtown streets. Progress had triumphed over fears that electricity

Charles Fletcher Lummis in 1885, at the conclusion of his trek from Ohio to California. *Courtesy of Keith Lummis.*

would contribute to blindness, harm ladies' complexions, attract lightning, and keep the chickens awake at night.

In 1885 Los Angeles gained a flamboyant new citizen: Charles Fletcher Lummis, who walked into town on February 1 after hiking 3,507 miles from Cincinnati. For the last eleven miles he was accompanied by his new employer, Harrison Gray Otis, whose *Los Angeles Daily Times* had begun publication in 1881. As author, editor, librarian, and collector, Lummis made valuable contributions to Los Angeles. He also left two remarkable landmarks. One is El Alisal, the house he built with his own hands on the west bank of the Arroyo Seco. The other is the great Southwest Museum, which towers above the Pasadena Freeway. Lummis founded the museum, bequeathed to it his books and artifacts, and influenced the design of the building.

Lummis described Los Angeles at the time of his arrival as a dull little town of about twelve thousand people. "The streets were narrow and crooked, with an infinite capacity for mud," he wrote. Third Street marked the edge of the business district, and beyond that, to the south, were "gardens and orchards and embowered residences." The look of the city was soon to change. By midsummer of 1886, Los Angeles was growing by about a thousand people a day, and orchards were giving way to town lots and subdivisions. It was the beginning of the great land boom of the eighties, fueled by extravagant publicity and by fierce competition between the Southern Pacific and the Santa Fe railroads. On November 29, 1885, the first Santa Fe train entered Los Angeles, ending a monopoly enjoyed by the Southern Pacific since 1876. The two lines soon engaged in a rate war. The price of tickets plummeted, and for a few hours on March 6, 1886,

Broadside advertising real estate opportunities during the boom of the eighties. The city's first electric railway extended from the Plaza to the subdivision. *Courtesy of Huntington Library.*

the fare from Kansas City, Missouri, to Los Angeles was just one dollar.

During the boom years some of the thousands of new arrivals came as winter visitors, but many more came to stay. With the increased demand for property, real estate values soared. A second wave of emigrants brought promoters and speculators: "to invest, wager or swindle," wrote Harris Newmark in *Sixty Years in Southern California*. Charles Lummis recalled a typical scene in Los Angeles in 1887. "At the tract office a line would begin to form one or two days before a sale was to open. I have seen many pay $100 for a place in that line . . . . Everyone was plunging–bankers, ministers, school teachers, policemen, tramps, judges, servant girls, bootblacks, car drivers, society ladies, counter jumpers."

The Boom peaked about August of 1887 and gradually subsided. "Yet not one single bank, not one well-established house, not one legitimate enterprise failed in the collapse of that stupendous madness," Lummis wrote. "For with all its greed, its ignorance, its idiocy, the boom was not quite a lottery. Thousands of lots were sold for far more than they were worth, but all were worth something real." The Boom resulted in a number of civic improvements. Downtown streets were paved, banks proliferated, and new high-rise buildings (a lofty four stories) were erected. Three new schools of higher education opened: Occidental College, the University of Southern California, and the State Normal School. Expensive homes and luxury hotels blossomed on hilltop sites, reached by modern cable car lines. As one historian observed, the Boom transformed a frontier town into a flourishing city.

Facing page: Entrance to Hale House.
Courtesy of Heritage Square Museum.

Heritage Square Museum

In 1884 J. J. Warner, who had settled in Los Angeles fifty years earlier, expressed pride in "this new, busy, bustling town of ours," but pointed out one consequence of urban growth. "Old landmarks are rapidly disappearing," he said. "Things which now are common, in a few years will be rare; and, after a few years more, will cease to be." Three-quarters of a century later, UCLA Chief Librarian Lawrence Clark Powell echoed Warner's words. "Going, going, gone," Powell wrote in a lament for vanished–or vanishing–links to the past: old railroad stations, packing houses, resort hotels, and splendid houses like those that once graced Bunker Hill. Shocked by the destruction of those old houses to make way for commercial development, in 1969 a group of citizens, working with the Los Angeles Cultural Heritage Board,

Palms Depot. *Photograph by Ralph E. Melching. Courtesy of Heritage Square Museum.*

established a haven for Victorian-era buildings threatened by demolition. That haven is Heritage Square Museum. A number of buildings, rescued from the bulldozer, have been brought together on the ten-acre museum site at 3800 Homer Street. Located on the east bank of the Arroyo Seco, in the Highland Park section of Los Angeles, it is about three miles north of the Los Angeles Civic Center.

Careful restoration of the exteriors and interiors of the museum's buildings is being carried forward by the Cultural Heritage Foundation of Southern California, Inc., and by a group of dedicated volunteers. Their mission is to preserve, restore, and interpret significant cultural and historic buildings of the late 19th century. The Heritage Square buildings date from 1876 to 1899 and include several homes, a carriage barn, a church, and a railroad depot.

The Palms Depot

In 1976 a little wooden depot that had served many generations of passengers made a journey of its own, traveling all night from its original site–five miles east of Santa Monica–to its new home in Heritage Square. The depot was erected by the Southern Pacific Railroad in 1887 in the boom town of The Palms. A contemporary account described the Palms Depot, with its Eastlake detailing, as "one of the most attractive in Southern California, nestled in a beautiful park, or rather, a cluster of parks." The subdividers boasted of planting thousands of trees–including palms–in the parks and along the sidewalks. "An air of good taste and permanency pervades all the improvements," said an approving news story.

William H. Perry Residence. *Courtesy of Heritage Square Museum.*

The depot served successively as a stop for Southern Pacific trains (1887 to 1908), Los Angeles Pacific trolleys (1908 to 1911), and the Pacific Electric's Big Red Cars (1911 to 1953). The line remained in place but was used only sporadically after 1953. The old depot gradually fell into disrepair and finally was condemned by the fire department. In 1975 the Cultural Heritage Foundation and a group of railroad enthusiasts raised the money needed to move the depot. Heading the fund-raising efforts was retired Disney animator Ward Kimball, who operated his own 3-foot gauge, full-size railroad in San Gabriel. On February 5, 1976, when the Foundation took possession of the Palms Depot, Kimball observed the occasion in appropriate fashion. Wearing a conductor's uniform and holding a kerosene lantern, he walked the rails one last time before the old station was moved to Heritage Square.

Sometime in the future the depot will again serve passengers. Plans are underway to build a trolley line through Heritage Square. Meanwhile, the depot serves as a visitor information center, and walking tours leave from the platform.

William H. Perry Residence
(Mount Pleasant House)

"Viewed from a distance," wrote Ludwig Salvator in 1876, "Los Angeles is entrancing from every angle. Perhaps the best view, however, is that from Mr. Perry's house and its charming garden in the foreground." He was referring to Mount Pleasant House, which stood on a hilltop in Boyle Heights and belonged to lumber magnate William H. Perry. As a young man Perry traveled

MUSEUMS ALONG THE ARROYO

Hale House. *Courtesy of Heritage Square Museum.*

with an overland party from Ohio to California. A penniless carpenter when he arrived, he soon opened a successful furniture store and later founded a prosperous lumber company with its own timberlands, ships, and docks. Perry helped organize the Los Angeles City Gas Company, and for twenty-five years was president of the Los Angeles City Water Company.

Stephen C. Hubbell, the second owner of Mount Pleasant House, was an attorney whose career included service as head of a street railway company, president of a bank, trustee of the University of Southern California, and member of the commission that helped lay out a park system for Los Angeles.

The last owner of Mount Pleasant House, before its move to Heritage Square, was the National Society of the Colonial Dames of America in California. The Colonial Dames play an active role nationwide in historic preservation. They saved Mount Pleasant House from demolition, moved it to Heritage Square in 1975, and funded extensive restoration of the building. In 1995 they donated the house and its contents to the museum. Accepting the gift, executive director Barry Herlihy described it as a magnificent addition to Heritage Square–"a place," he said, "where history is brought to life."

Mount Pleasant House is on the National Register of Historic Places. An outstanding example of Italianate style, it was designed in 1876 by Ezra F. Kysor.

Hale House

Hale House, built around 1887 in Highland Park, stood for almost a hundred years along the main route between Los Angeles and Pasadena. The builder–and

Valley Knudsen Garden Residence.
Courtesy of Heritage Square Musum.

probably the first resident–was George Washington Morgan, a real estate dealer and developer. After a succession of owners, the house was purchased in 1906 by James G. Hale and his wife, Bessie. The Hales eventually separated, but Bessie continued to live in the house, occupying it for a longer period than any previous owner. In 1970 Hale House was moved about five blocks–to Heritage Square from North Figueroa Street and Avenue 45.

Hale House is a notable example of Queen Anne architecture with Eastlake detailing. The house has a corner turret, ornate brick chimneys, iron grillwork, and stained glass windows. The exterior colors–four shades of green, three of red, with black and yellow trim–were reproduced from chips of the original colors. The interior has been fully restored and contains furnishings of the period, including a William Morris recliner. The dining room, restored under the sponsorship of Les Dames of Los Angeles, has received many awards for authenticity. Hale House is on the National Register of Historic Places.

VALLEY KNUDSEN GARDEN RESIDENCE
(SHAW HOUSE)

Around 1883, cabinetmaker Richard E. Shaw built a Mansard-style cottage with Queen Anne detailing. Originally located on Mozart Street, in Lincoln Heights, the house later was moved to nearby Johnston Street. In 1971 it was moved again–this time to Heritage Square–to save the house from demolition. Restoration of the cottage has been made possible by a generous grant from the Tom and Valley Knudsen Foundation. To honor the

Stable and carriage barn. *Photograph by Doris Arima.
Courtesy of Heritage Square Museum.*

founder of Los Angeles Beautiful, the house has been named the Valley Knudsen Garden Residence. It is on the National Register of Historic Places.

A handsome coral tree (the official tree of Los Angeles) shades the cottage. The Bel Air Garden Club arranged to have the tree moved from its previous location on Johnston Street. The Club also funded the planting of a period rose garden.

When Richard Shaw built his cottage, the roof was crowned with a cupola, but this was removed many years before the move to Heritage Square. Guided by old photographs, woodshop students at Eagle Rock High School reproduced the cupola, which was installed in 1982.

The museum store–which is known as Mrs. Shaw's Emporium–presently occupies the first floor of the cottage. Its inventory includes antiques, jewelry, jams and jellies, children's games, and a wide assortment of books on art, architecture, and Southern California history.

Carriage Barn

Built in 1899 as a stable and carriage barn, and later converted to a dwelling and garage, the old barn now houses the museum's restoration and maintenance workshops. The little building is a mixture of Queen Anne Cottage and Gothic styles. It was located on property acquired by the Huntington Memorial Hospital when it expanded along California Street in Pasadena. To make way for a new parking lot, the hospital donated the carriage barn to Heritage Square in 1981.

Longfellow-Hastings Octagon House on its original site.
Courtesy of Heritage Square Museum.

HERITAGE SQUARE MUSEUM

Longfellow-Hastings Octagon House

After ninety-three years as the home of one Pasadena family, the only octagon house in Southern California was moved to Heritage Square. The house was built in 1893 by Gilbert Longfellow, who previously had built an octagon house in his native Maine. Orson S. Fowler's *A Home for All*, first published in 1848, championed octagonal structures as cheaper to build, easier to heat and ventilate, and letting in more sunlight than the conventional square or rectangle. The subtitle to later editions of his best-selling book summed up the octagon's advantages: "New, Cheap, Convenient, Superior and Adapted to Rich and Poor."

The Longfellow-Hastings House has two stories, a central staircase, and an eight-sided cupola on a hipped roof. There are four square rooms on each floor. Corner angles accomodated the entryway, pantry, bathrooms, and closets. The octagon house originally stood on San Pasqual Avenue in Pasadena but was moved in 1917 to nearby South Allen Avenue. The last owner was Gilbert Longfellow's grandson, Walter Hastings. When he moved from Pasadena in 1986, he gave the old family home to Heritage Square Museum, to be preserved and restored. Books and photographs that came with the house have been added to the Museum's research library. With his gift Hastings made only one proviso. "My family were agricultural, farming people, living simply," he said. "The house is to be furnished without frills."

The Longfellow-Hastings House is on the National Register of Historic Places.

MUSEUMS ALONG THE ARROYO

John J. Ford House. *Photograph by Bruce Boehner.
Courtesy of Heritage Square Museum.*

HERITAGE SQUARE MUSEUM

John J. Ford House

The John J. Ford House, named for its first owner, was built about 1887 on Beaudry Avenue, near Third, in downtown Los Angeles. The architecture combines Italianate, Eastlake, and Queen Anne styles. Ford, who was a prolific wood carver, added extensive handcarved details to both the exterior and the interior. He also did carvings for the veterans hospital in West Los Angeles, the California State Capitol, Leland Stanford's private railroad car, Stanford University's Memorial Church, St. Vibiana's Cathedral, the Mormon Temple in Salt Lake City, and the Iolani Palace on Oahu.

Ford's only son, William Joseph, was chief deputy district attorney during the trial of the McNamara brothers for the bombing of the *Los Angeles Times*. He later became the first dean of the Loyola University Law School. J. J. Ford's oldest daughter, Eleanor, married a son of the grape grower, vintner, and horse breeder L. J. Rose, for whom the city of Rosemead is named.

In 1974 the Bank of America purchased the site of the Ford House to build a data processing center, and it donated the little house to Heritage Square Museum. At one time the house was converted to a duplex, then to a number of efficiency apartments. The original floorplan is now restored. Dr. Herbert Williams, J. J. Ford's grandson, has supplied valuable information about the house and has been instrumental in raising funds for its restoration.

South of Ford House, along the edge of the Arroyo, the museum has planted a small orange grove, symbolizing the importance of the citrus industry in 19th century Southern California. The Museum also is developing the

Lincoln Avenue Methodist Church. *Photograph by Doris Arima. Courtesy of Heritage Square Museum.*

Ford House Kitchen Garden. It is based on a plan designed by Robert Smaus, editor of the *Los Angeles Times* Garden Section. The plan calls for flower beds, as well as vegetable beds, and for such domestic amenities as a backyard clothesline. ("Every garden had one," says Smaus.)

LINCOLN AVENUE METHODIST CHURCH

In 1897 Pasadena Methodists laid the cornerstone for a church at Lincoln and Orange Grove avenues. Perry M. Green, one of the colonists who settled in Pasadena in 1874, gave the invocation. The designer of Lincoln Avenue Methodist Church was New York architect George W. Kramer, who specialized in church design. Pasadena architect Will A. Benshoff supervised construction of the new church, a fine example of Carpenter Gothic, with Eastlake detailing. The building has large circular windows set in gable arches, classical pediments over each of the three entrances, and a partial Arroyo boulder foundation. Over the main corner entrance is an octagonal steeple, twenty-one feet tall. Worshippers attended services at Lincoln Avenue Methodist Church for seventy years. Membership gradually declined, however, and in 1967 the old church was converted to the Lincoln Social Center. Among the services it offered were job referrals, a day care center, a Discovery School for young children, and a senior citizens recreational facility.

In 1980 the U.S. Postal Service acquired the site for a general mail facility. Recognizing the historic significance of the church, the postal service and the city of Pasadena donated funds to move it to Heritage Square for restoration and preservation. The venerable redwood

Proposed layout for interior of "The Colonial Drug. George A. Simmons, Proprietor." *Rendering by George A. Terpatsi. Courtesy of Heritage Square Museum.*

structure arrived at its new home on Lincoln's birthday in 1981. In August of that year the old cornerstone was relaid with its original contents: a Bible, a hymnal, two sheets of blueprints, and copies of four newspapers published in 1897. The partially restored building provides space for a temporary exhibits gallery and for apprenticeship classes sponsored by the Plasterers Union, which has contributed its services for several museum projects.

The Colonial Drug

Heritage Square Museum helps bring to life the domestic, cultural, and economic history of Los Angeles in the 19th and early 20th centuries. To complement its residential and transportation exhibits, the museum is planning its first commercial exhibit: the accurate re-creation of a corner drugstore, complete with working soda fountain. The building, to be erected by Heritage Square Museum, will feature the Colonial Drug Collection. This consists of antique apothecary items, as well as drugstore fixtures and displays from the 1890s. The material was donated by Frederick L. and Sidney M. Simmons. Their father–George A. Simmons–began his career as a druggist around 1912 in China, continued it in the United States, and founded The Colonial Drug in Highland Park in 1927.

The drugstore and its historic collection will be of interest to pharmacists, as well as the general public, and will further the museum's ongoing program to create a living history site that opens a window on the past.

Facing page: Lummis Home doorway.
Photograph by Tom M. Apostol.

El Alisal:
The Lummis Home

Across the Arroyo Seco from Heritage Square is El Alisal, the house that Charles Fletcher Lummis built to last one thousand years. Its architecture, he wrote, "is part of my life and my brains and my love and my hands." As the site for his house, Lummis chose three acres a few miles from downtown Los Angeles, at 200 East Avenue 43 in Highland Park. Describing his property he said, "It was covered with brush, gravel, granite boulders and thirty noble sycamores." A magnificent tree with a fourfold trunk inspired the name El Alisal: the local Spanish for Place of the Sycamore.

Lummis started work on El Alisal in 1898. Not yet forty years old, he already had made a name for himself as first city editor of the *Los Angeles Times*; editor of the monthly journal, *Land of Sunshine*; author of ten books; photographer of the Southwest, Mexico, and South America; and founder of the Landmarks Club, which

MUSEUMS ALONG THE ARROYO

Photograph by Charles Lummis showing El Alisal under construction in 1898. *Courtesy of Huntington Library.*

worked to rescue from decay California's old Franciscan missions. He went on to distinguish himself as Los Angeles City Librarian, founder of the Southwest Museum, and founder of the Sequoyah League, whose goal was to change the government's Indian policy.

While involved in many of these projects he also was busy constructing El Alisal, the L-shaped house he painstaking erected around the giant sycamore. Lummis called the house his stone castle. Made of concrete and faced with Arroyo boulders, it boasts a circular tower thirty feet tall, a scroll-topped bell cote, and lattice-work chimneys like one at Mission San Juan Capistrano. Lummis did most of the work on El Alisal himself: hauling boulders, laying foundations, putting up walls, and fashioning cupboards, shelves, and doors. "The creative thrill is so fine and keen," he said, "it is sheer pitiful to see a man get a home off the bargain counter, and miss nearly all the joy he might just as well have of it."

Lummis often worked from daybreak till dark on the construction of El Alisal. In the process he learned new skills. "Damn plastering flies everywhere but to the wall, at first," he admitted on one occasion, "but presently I get it tame and to stick to the wall–and feel right proud." Each year one or two young boys from Isleta Pueblo helped with some of the tasks (Lummis had spent four years in the Pueblo); and for specialized jobs like masonry he turned to professionals. He also worked closely with Sumner Hunt, an architectural advisor to the Landmarks Club and later chief architect of the Southwest Museum.

As Lummis described his house in a letter written in 1912 to the Los Angeles Park Commission:

The El Alisal *museo*, in which Lummis displayed his collections.
Courtesy of Keith Lummis.

EL ALISAL: THE LUMMIS HOME

The woodwork is massive and all by hand–no mill work. The ceiling beams are 8" x 10" and 10" x 12", all hewn by me with the broad ax; except two rooms where there are 12-inch cedar logs burned and rubbed. The ceilings are 3-inch redwood, hewn by me with the adze. The casings are massive, no two doors or windows alike; all hewn. Front door weighs a ton. Thinnest door three inches thick. Mostly dovetailed. Floors cement, ceilings fireproofed. Choice woods. Many historic timbers and other articles built in.

The first room that Lummis built–and the largest–is the *museo*, a combination of living room and exhibition hall. Here he displayed his Indian blankets, baskets, pots, and other artifacts, as well as his many paintings by Western artists. Most of the collections now are in the Southwest Museum, but a number of personal items are exhibited in the *museo*. Among them are photographs of friends and family, the machine used by Lummis to make wax-cylinder recordings, and his typewriter with moveable type.

The ceiling beams in the *museo* and adjoining entrance hall are utility poles obtained from the Santa Fe Railroad. Like the rest of the house, the *museo* has plastered walls and concrete floors. "Housecleaning has no terrors here," said Lummis, who advised hosing down the interior when it was dirty. An outstanding feature of the *museo* is its photographic window. Its three large panes are bordered with black and white glass transparencies made from photographs taken by Lummis in the Southwestern United States, Mexico, Bolivia, and Peru.

Even before finishing the *museo*, Lummis began work on the *zaguán*, the entrance hall adjoining it on the east. He was proud of the careful dovetailing in the door

Lummis as portrayed by Alexander Harmer on a page of the House Book signed by guests at El Alisal. *Courtesy of Southwest Museum, Los Angeles. N 41959.*

between *zaguán* and patio. "Any fool can write a book," he often remarked, "but it takes a man to make a dovetail door." A gift from Bishop George Montgomery–a plank from Mission San Fernando–adds interest to another door in the *zaguán*. Writing about the gift, Lummis reported: "Panel just as it was hewn by the padres in 1797; but was for 50 years over the smoke-room where they smoked their hams; and it is indurated almost like a fossil."

For a brief time the *zaguán* served as Lummis's office, with a William Keith painting on the wall and a roll-top desk the chief item of furniture. The room was the setting for the first wedding at El Alisal: that of Maynard and Lillian Dixon in 1905. A table in the *zaguán* held the great red morocco house book signed by the Dixons and hundreds of other visitors to El Alisal. Artists, actors, writers, musicians, ethnologists, and historians were among those who autographed or illustrated some of the four hundred pages in the book. A few of the familiar names to be found here are those of John Muir, Will Rogers, Helena Modjeska, Carl Sandburg, Frederic Remington, and John Philip Sousa. Cowboy artist Ed Borein drew several sketches in the house book, including one made on his wedding day, when he and Lucile Maxwell were married at El Alisal. (The original copy of the house book now is in the Southwest Museum.)

The great front entrance into the *zaguán* is nearly seven feet high with massive double doors, each half weighing about a thousand pounds. The planks are made of yellow pine and red birch ("our native mahogany") and fastened with wrought-iron nails. An expedition that Lummis made to Peru and Bolivia with archaeologist

A corner of "The Lion's Den." The cabinet, which held Lummis's camera, has a design pyrographed by Maynard Dixon.
Courtesy of Southwest Museum, Los Angeles. N24262.

EL ALISAL: THE LUMMIS HOME

Adolph Bandelier inspired the designs of the impressive hardware. The flowing calligraphic device is a copy of the flourish–or *rúbrica*–that conquistador Francisco Pizarro used with his signature. The hinges resemble the condor-headed sceptres carried by a pre-Incan deity. Lummis had photographed a stone carving of the god on a monumental gateway at Tiahuanaco, in the Andes. El Alisal's splendid double doors, completed in the spring of 1899, were used for little more than a year. Then they were locked and bolted, a symbol of the grief that closed in on Lummis when his six-year-old son Amado died on Christmas Day of 1900.

The little guest room east of the *zaguán* is notable for its fireplace, on which Charles Walter Stetson modeled a Navajo fire dance. Lummis composed the couplet inscribed around the fireplace opening:

A casual savage cracked two stones together:
A spark–and Man was armed against the weather.

By 1901 Lummis had finished a bedroom, bathroom, and vestibule at the eastern end of the house. He designed the bedroom for Eve Lummis, his second wife, and gave it a tiny alcove that he called Eve's tower. After completing the room, Lummis turned his attention to a plumbing project. "Build that noble bathtub," he wrote in his journal, "and it took 2 mighty good men 12 hours steady labor, interrupted only twice for 20-minute bites of meals. But it will be just the same bathtub 10,000 years from now. I wish the plumbing and the pipes and the nickel plating would last as long!"

A doorway in the vestibule opens onto the veranda; and a steep, narrow staircase leads to the second floor, where Lummis built his daughter Turbesé's bedroom, his

A Lummis photograph of the dining room. The lamps were made from Indian baskets and fringed with buckskin.
Courtesy of Historical Society of Southern California.

EL ALISAL: THE LUMMIS HOME

own study, an attic, and the upper story to the tower. "It's a beauty," Lummis proudly said of his upstairs study. This was the famous "Lion's Den" in which he did his writing. "On one side of the study," wrote a visitor in 1905, "a narrow hole opens into an unfinished attic. Through this hole and the attic Mr. Lummis crawls to his bedchamber in the tower." Barbed wire reinforced the tower walls, a two-thousand-pound girder strengthened the floor, and twenty boulders, each weighing two hundred and fifty pounds, served as battlements. When the Southwest Museum was built, Lummis had a splendid view of its tower from one of his own tower windows.

It was not until 1904 that Lummis finished work on the west wing of El Alisal: dining room, pantry and kitchen. The spacious dining room, or *comedor,* (almost as large as the *museo*) has a corner fireplace, wall niches like those in a pueblo dwelling, and an open-beamed ceiling with corbels and herringbone planking. In the floor by the fireplace are six diamond-shaped tiles arranged to form a star. The tiles came from the ruined old Mission San Juan Capistrano, whose roof and adobe walls were repaired by Lummis's Landmarks Club. Next to the fireplace is a woodbox made by Lummis and decorated by artist Maynard Dixon, who pyrographed the Indian motifs of a bird, a deer, and a bear.

Lummis made several interesting pieces of furniture for the *comedor.* One cupboard has heavy shelves hewn to fit securely into wedge-shaped notches. A sideboard incorporates "a precious pair of cupboard doors" carved from Spanish cedar in the early eighteenth century. Lummis brought the old doors from Isleta Pueblo in 1900 and built them into the upper part of his sideboard. As

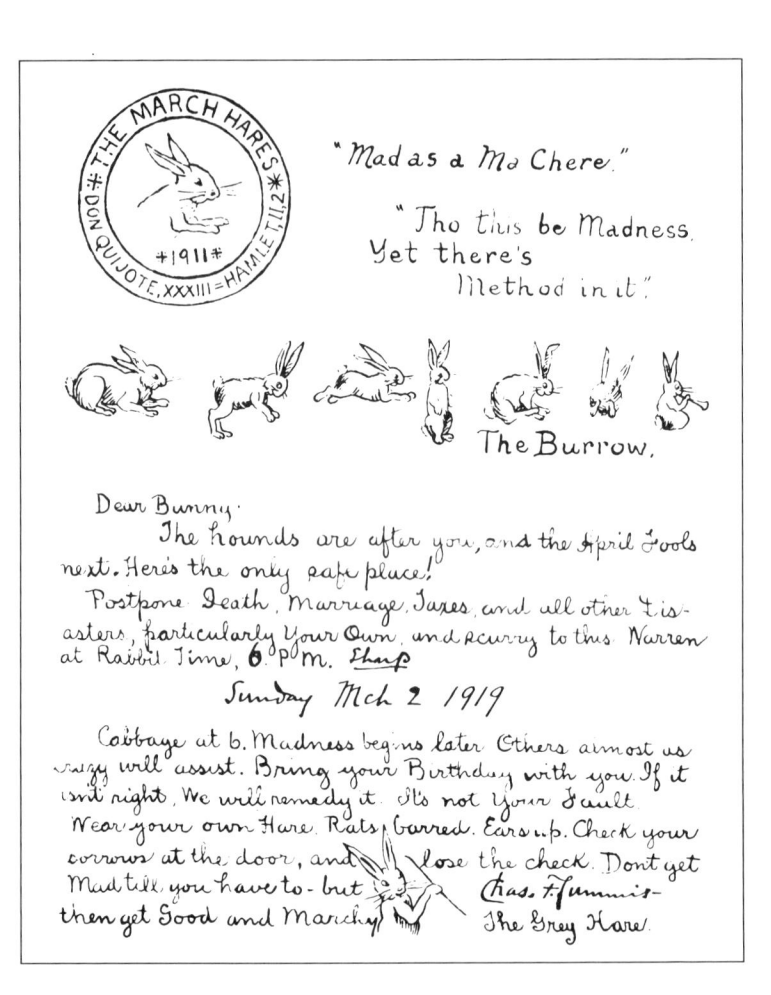

> **"Mad as a Ma Chere."**
>
> **"Tho this be Madness, Yet there's Method in it."**
>
> The Burrow.
>
> Dear Bunny:
> The hounds are after you, and the April Fools next. Here's the only safe place! Postpone Death, Marriage, Taxes, and all other Disasters, particularly Your Own, and scurry to this Warren at Rabbit Time, 6. p.m. Sharp
>
> Sunday Mch 2 1919
>
> Cabbage at 6. Madness begins later. Others almost as crazy will assist. Bring your Birthday with you. If it isn't right, We will remedy it. It's not Your fault. Wear your own Hare. Rats, barred. Ears up. Check your sorrows at the door, and lose the check. Don't get Mad till you have to – but then get Good and Marchy.
>
> Chas. F. Lummis —
> The Grey Hare.

Invitation to a party honoring friends with birthdays in March.
Courtesy of Southwest Museum, Los Angeles. N24539

with much of his other carpentry, both sideboard and cupboard show the mark of the adze. No friend of the planing mill, as one reporter observed, Lummis preferred an irregular surface and the wavy effect that he called a moonlight finish.

Some lively dinner parties took place in the *comedor*. For a number of years Lummis played host to members of the Order of the Mad March Hares: friends with birthdays in March. Often he entertained at what he called "Noises" and defined as an "informal Old California Good Time." Journalist Harry Carr offered another definition: "shindig of the intellectuals."

On the swinging door between dining room and pantry is a huge slice of redwood burl, a birthday gift from artist Fernand Lungren. The pantry is conveniently arranged, with many shelves, two pass-throughs for dishes, and an air-cooler for food. The kitchen, patterned after one at Mission San Juan Capistrano, took seven months to build. The walls (reinforced with barbed wire) slope upward to a vent in the high ceiling. A steep flight of stairs goes from the kitchen to the basement wine cellar, which was well stocked with claret and sauterne. One of the kitchen doors leads to the pantry, one to the patio, and a third to what Lummis described as "a nice screen breakfast room on the porch–all screen and morning glories." The porch area since has been enclosed.

In a climate where it was possible to enjoy the outdoors for at least 325 days a year, said Lummis, any well-planned house should have a patio and veranda, and he wrote articles in praise of both. The veranda at El Alisal (offering "spacious, gracious, airy coolness") extends for fifty feet along the north side of the house and is presided

Lummis at work with his wood chisel in 1901. *Courtesy of Southwest Museum, Los Angeles. N13527.*

EL ALISAL: THE LUMMIS HOME

over by a mural of a young Isleta girl by a heap of drying corn. The mural–possibly done by Charles Russell–is similar to a picture taken by Lummis in 1888 and later incorporated in the photographic window of the *museo*.

The magisterial sycamore named *El Alcade Mayor,* or the Chief Justice, once dominated the patio at El Alisal. Numerous social events–including Lummis's third wedding–took place beneath the sycamore's great canopy. In the name of *El Alcade Mayor* Lummis issued subpoenas and conducted mock trials of "Hardened & Notorious Sinners" accused of "the High Misdemeanor of Not Knowing An Old California Good Time." Those receiving a summons were told: "The prosecutor is Fierce, but the Jury of 18 has been Carefully Packed in Your Favor. If you can put up any sort of defense the verdict will be 'Not Guilty, Come Again.'"

With the construction of dining room and kitchen, the house was essentially complete by 1904. Asked, however, when he expected the work to end, Lummis replied, *"Never,* I hope." As he explained to archaeologist Frederick Webb Hodge, the demands of deskwork made physical labor a necessary and welcome counterpoint. "By it," he said, "I keep in good trim. Without it I sh[oul]d be dead in six months." He still had plans to build another room and a seventy-foot cloister. He also wanted to make his own tiles with which to roof El Alisal. Although he carried out none of these projects, he did build two small guest houses across the patio from the main house.

"I have made a beautiful home worthy for my children to live in, and fit to be lived in for a thousand years," Lummis wrote in 1910 in a preamble to his will. To pro-

El Alisal photographed by Lummis in 1905 to show his landscape of wildflowers. *Courtesy of Southwest Museum, Los Angeles. N22042*

EL ALISAL: THE LUMMIS HOME

tect members of his family "against their own improvidence or misfortune in the future," he conveyed El Alisal to the Southwest Museum to hold in trust for his children and their descendants, "as a home and residence; subject only to the right of the public to free view of the exhibit rooms three hours a week."

Lummis assumed that deeding El Alisal to the Southwest Museum would allow his children, and those who came after them, to live tax-free and rent-free, with land enough to support them. In 1923, however, the museum decided it was neither legal nor practical to commit itself to maintaining a home for the family in perpetuity. The museum did keep El Alisal for a number of years after Lummis's death in 1928, and two generations of the family continued to live there.

In 1939 the state acquired a narrow strip on the eastern edge of the property for a street extension. At about the same time the Southwest Museum announced that it could no longer afford the upkeep of El Alisal and must sell both house and land. Preservationists rallied to save the property as a historic landmark, and in 1941 the legislature voted funds to acquire El Alisal. Title passed in 1943 from the museum to the state, which named the property California State Monument No. 531. The city of Los Angeles leased El Alisal from 1944 until 1971, when it became the legal owner.

Since 1965 the Historical Society of Southern California (HSSC) has had its headquarters in El Alisal. One of its major projects has been redesign of the garden area to demonstrate the use of drought-tolerant plants in a residential setting. "The garden keeps us from being a museum that just displays the past," says HSSC execu-

El Alisal in 1986, after work began on renovation of the garden. *Photograph by Harry Chamberlain. Courtesy of Historical Society of Southern California.*

EL ALISAL: THE LUMMIS HOME

tive director Thomas F. Andrews. "It gives us a chance to be a real living force for the future." Robert C. Perry, professor of landscape architecture at Cal Poly Pomona, designed the Lummis Home Water-Conserving Garden. "I tried to complement the nature of the site," he stated, "but also be sensitive to the fabric of this region in terms of its climate, soils, and plant communities." Since its dedication in 1987, the garden has won several awards and attracted thousands of visitors to El Alisal.

HSSC sponsors a number of special events at the Lummis Home, including book talks, autograph parties, special exhibits, and an annual garden fair. The Society offers guided tours of the house and garden; and it maintains the El Alisal Book Shop, which offers a large selection of books and pamphlets on gardening, as well as on California and the West. The house continues to reflect the personality of its builder and his interest in the old missions of California, the pueblos of the American Southwest, and the archaeology of Mexico, Bolivia, and Peru.

Facing page: The museum's tunnel entrance before its restoration in 1996. *Photograph by Tom M. Apostol.*

The Southwest Museum

In February 1895 Charles Fletcher Lummis, the new editor of *Land of Sunshine*, began campaigning for a museum in Los Angeles. "The vital point," he wrote, "is that there should be a museum here–and before it shall be too late to acquire the best that such a museum will ever get."

His dream was realized on August 1, 1914, when the Southwest Museum opened to the public in a towering Mission Revival building at Marmion Way and Museum Drive.

Lummis took the first steps toward founding a museum when the Archaeological Institute of America asked him in 1903 to start a Los Angeles branch of the organization, whose headquarters were in Boston. He promptly launched the Southwest Society of the Institute and proclaimed, "We want a Museum in Los Angeles–not an old Curiosity Shop of jumbles from God-knows-where, but a Museum which can compare with any in the world in everything but bulk." Within a year the Southwest

A Lummis photograph of Rosendo Uruchurtu making a wax-cylinder recording for the museum collection. *Courtesy of Southwest Museum, Los Angeles. N24310.*

THE SOUTHWEST MUSEUM

Society had acquired two valuable collections of early California material and had begun its efforts to preserve *Californio* and Native American Indian songs by recording them on wax cylinders. ("Catching Our Archaeology Alive" was Lummis's imaginative phrase for the music project.)

The fledgling Southwest Museum incorporated in 1907. At the same time it made plans to build in Highland Park on a spectacular hilltop site, "an acropolis in the valley of the Arroyo Seco," which commanded views from the San Gabriel Mountains to the sea. Lummis chose the site, and attorney Henry W. O'Melveny raised the money to purchase it.

Until the museum was built, its collections were on public view in Los Angeles: first in the Pacific Electric Building at Sixth and Main and then in M. A. Hamburger's huge department store at Eighth and Broadway. (The museum displayed its collections on the sixth floor of the Hamburger Building, the Los Angeles Public Library occupied the third floor, and the library's garden reading room–an innovation of City Librarian Charles Lummis–was on the roof.)

Ground-breaking for the Southwest Museum took place on November 16, 1912. During the ceremonies Elizabeth Benton Frémont unfurled the hand-sewn flag that her father, John Charles Frémont, had raised on a snow-capped peak in the Rockies on his first Western expedition. A year after the ground-breaking, the museum cornerstone was laid. Incised on the stone is the drawing of an ancient artifact in the shape of a bird. Encircling it are the words *Mañana Flor de Sus Ayeres*– Tomorrow is the flower of its yesterdays. The bird design

MUSEUMS ALONG THE ARROYO

The Southwest Museum around 1920, when the elevator was under construction. In the foreground is one of the yellow trolley cars of the Los Angeles Railway. *Courtesy of Southwest Museum, Los Angeles. N32167.*

and the Spanish motto, which were suggested by Lummis, appeared on the museum's corporate seal.

The chief architect for the Southwest Museum was Sumner Hunt, who had advised the Landmarks Club on preservation of the missions and had advised Lummis during the building of El Alisal. Lummis worked with Hunt on every detail of the museum, from the location of exhibit cases to the design of the great seven-story caracol tower, with its spiral staircase of 160 steps. The tower was named in honor of Lummis ("Founder Emeritus") on the occasion of his sixty-fourth birthday.

On July 26, 1914, the museum collections were moved from the Hamburger Building into their new home, and the Southwest Museum opened to the public six days later. Hiking up to the museum's hilltop entrance proved daunting for many visitors, so a lower entrance was constructed in 1920. Portals ornamented with Mayan motifs open to a corridor 240 feet long and lined with a series of miniature dioramas depicting Native American Indian life. The corridor leads to an elevator that carries passengers up 108 feet to the first-floor level of the museum.

The museum's upper entrance is reached by a narrow winding road for automobiles or by a pedestrian path, "the Hopi Trail." The steep trail ends at the museum's Ethnobotanical Garden, which features plants used by the California native peoples for food, shelter, medicine, and tools, as well as for basketry and musical instruments.

Visitors who prefer to drive to the upper entrance will find ample parking and a bird's-eye view of the Arroyo. Alongside steps to the patio and the museum entrance is a red cedar totem pole twenty feet high. It was carved

"Apache Spirit," which combines references to modern technology and traditional Apache designs. The steel sculpture, by Bob Haozous, was placed near the entrance to the Southwest Museum in 1988. *Photograph by Tom M. Apostol.*

especially for the Southwest Museum by two artists from Vancouver Island: Richard Hunt of the Kwa-Gulth (Kwakiutl) people, and Tim Paul of the Nuu-Chah-Nulth (Nootka) people. Another monumental work of art that greets the visitor is "Apache Spirit," a sheet-steel sculpture by Bob Haozous, a Chiricahua Apache. The huge sculpture combines a traditional Apache design with references to modern technology.

The Southwest Museum contains some of the finest examples in the United States of Native American Indian materials. It also has important holdings of Mesoamerican and South American Precolumbian pottery and textiles, as well as Hispanic folk and decorative arts. In addition to a changing exhibits gallery, the museum has four permanent exhibit halls and a permanent display, in open storage, of about 500 baskets, out of some 11,000 owned by the museum. (More than 20 percent of the baskets had belonged to a discerning private collector, Caroline Boeing Poole. They were donated to the museum in 1939.)

As currently arranged, the museum's four exhibit halls present the native cultures of the Great Plains, the Southwest, California, and the Northwest Coast. The focal point of the Plains Hall is a Cheyenne summer tipi. Among the items displayed in the cases are beaded moccasins, a painted buffalo robe, and a child's robe decorated with quills. Presiding over the Southwest Hall are five life-size models wearing Navajo blankets woven around 1850. Also on display are kachinas, jewelry, baskets, and some of the museum's 7,000 pottery vessels. At the entrance to the California Hall is the replica of a Chumash painted cave. The surrounding cases hold

George Wharton James examining baskets at his home in Pasadena. The Southwest Museum has extensive holdings of the baskets, pottery, textiles, and other artifacts that James collected over a period of more than forty years. *Courtesy of Southwest Museum, Los Angeles. N29461.*

remarkable examples of basketry. They range from the practical (such as those involved in acorn processing) to the purely aesthetic (a Pomo basket so small it is viewed through a magnifying glass). The Northwest Coast Hall has a huge totemic painting of Beaver at the entrance and two enormous carved and painted Haida houseposts at the rear of the hall. The display cases contain such items as a rattle in the shape of a raven, a halibut hook that is both artistic and functional, and a potlatch basketry hat. Miniature dioramas in the various halls set the scene for added appreciation of the artifacts on exhibit and the people who made them.

Only a fraction of the museum's holdings can be displayed at any one time. Duane H. King, appointed as museum director in 1995, plans to refurbish the exhibits, supplement them with interactive audiovisuals, and emphasize the cultural context of how an artifact was used or what its function was in society. He says of the Southwest Museum, "It is poised to become one of the nation's premier museums in the twenty-first century."

Throughout the year the museum offers guided gallery tours, by reservation, for student and adult groups. In addition it offers a lively series of special events, including an Intertribal Marketplace, films, festivals, workshops, storytelling, and demonstrations by noted artists. The Museum Store carries handcrafted items and a wide selection of publications.

Braun Research Library

By 1910 the newly incorporated Southwest Museum had received two important gifts, the nucleus of its great research library. The donors were Dr. Joseph Amasa

Annie Healing, Nampeyo's daughter, photographed by A.C. Vroman in 1901 at Hano, First Mesa. Vroman acquired several of the pots, and they were donated to the Southwest Museum in 1917. The museum owns some 120,000 photographs, including many by Vroman. *Courtesy of Southwest Museum, Los Angeles. N20698.*

Munk, who gave thousands of items of Arizoniana; and Charles Fletcher Lummis, who bequeathed his books, personal papers, manuscripts, photographs, and music to the museum and also established an endowment to acquire publications in his areas of interest. (A drawing of Lummis, in the guise of an Indian fire-maker, appears on the bookplate designed for the Munk Library of Arizoniana.)

The Southwest Museum's Braun Research Library occupies its own building, which was erected in 1977 on the museum courtyard. Construction was made possible by a gift from museum president C. Allan Braun. For the library entrance, sculptor Erwin Binder created a symbolic representation of Sequoyah, honored as the inventor of a system for writing the Cherokee language.

The Braun Research Library is a major center for information on the archaeology and anthropology of the Americas and the history of the American West. Its extensive holdings include prints, drawings, and photographs; incunabula and other rare books; more than 50,000 reference books; and an archive of sound recordings. The manuscript collection contains the personal papers of such notable Westerners as Charles Fletcher Lummis, Frederick Webb Hodge, George Wharton James, and Edward S. Curtis. The reading room is dedicated to Carl S. Denzel, director of the museum from 1955 to 1980.

Casa de Adobe

The museum's Spanish Colonial collections are housed in the Casa de Adobe, which is on Figueroa Street, several blocks from the museum. The Casa was

Performers at an early Fiesta held at the Casa de Adobe. *Courtesy of Southwest Museum, Los Angeles. N32147.*

built by the Hispanic Society of Los Angeles as an example of a wealthy family's home in California's rancho period. Construction was completed in December 1918, and the property was transferred to the Southwest Museum in 1925. The building, designed by Theodore Eisen, was inspired to a great extent by the adobe on Rancho Guajome, located a few miles from Mission San Luis Rey in San Diego County. The Casa de Adobe has eight reconstructed period rooms built around a central patio. The house is a colorful setting for special museum programs, including the annual holiday presentation of Las Posadas.

The Southwest Museum is the oldest museum in Los Angeles. Conceived in 1903, incorporated in 1907, and opened to the public in 1914, it has worked for nearly a century to preserve and interpret Native American Indian and Hispanic cultures. Through its world-famous collection of artifacts, its great research library, and its adjunct museum, the Casa de Adobe, it continues to fulfill its purpose: "To educate, enlighten, and enrich."

Facing page: Crest of the Arroyo Guild, emblazoned over the main entrance of The Judson Studios. *Photograph by Tom M. Apostol.*

Along The Arroyo Seco

"A winding, romantic strip of wild-wood," said an admirer of the Arroyo Seco, writing in an 1894 newspaper. One hundred and twenty-five years earlier, Miguel Costansó, engineer and cartographer with the Portolá expedition, described the Arroyo with more precision. His diary for August 2, 1769, referred to a beautiful river (we know it as the Los Angeles River) and to "another water-course or river-bed which formed a wide ravine, but it was dry. This water-course joined that of the river, and gave clear indications of heavy floods during the rainy season, as it had many branches of trees and debris on its banks." It was an accurate description of the Arroyo Seco, the usually dry stream bed that originates in the San Gabriel Mountains and extends to the Los Angeles River.

Pasadena author, naturalist, and sportsman Charles Frederick Holder, writing in the 1880s, contrasted the summertime appearance of the Arroyo ("the bed of a lit-

MUSEUMS ALONG THE ARROYO

The Arroyo Seco after the devastating floods of 1914. In the background is the Southwest Museum under construction. *Courtesy of Southwest Museum, Los Angeles, N37694.*

tle stream which now and then disappears") with its winter aspect ("after a rain, bearing in its tortuous channel a rushing torrent of great power"). Hikers and equestrians, he said, would find in the Arroyo "lofty sycamores, overhung with wild grape, clematis and creepers of various kinds–a veritable jungle of midwinter growth, in which the harmless wildcat and coyote make their lair and the black-tailed deer occasionally strays."

The beauty of the Arroyo deeply impressed novelist Mary Austin. "At most seasons of the year," she wrote, "[it is] a small trickle of water among stones in a wide, deep wash, overgrown with button willows and sycamores. . . . Tiny gold and silver backed ferns climb down the banks to drink, and as soon as the spring freshet has gone by, brodiaeas and blazing stars come up between the boulders worn as smooth as if by hand."

Theodore Roosevelt, visiting the area in 1911, was just as impressed. Instead of waxing poetic, however, he thundered: "This Arroyo would make one of the greatest parks in the world!" He made the remark to his old Harvard schoolmate, Charles Fletcher Lummis. A few years later Lummis became a founding board member of the Arroyo Seco Association, "organized to protect the most beautiful Valley in the City of Los Angeles from devastation by flood or fire, and from disfigurement by factories or in any other way; and to preserve the natural beauties of the Arroyo, and to improve them as far as possible." Areas on either side of the watercourse have since been declared as parkland, but the watercourse itself has been tamed and confined for much of its length, transformed into a concrete flood control channel.

At the turn of the century an extraordinary group of

USC's College of Fine Arts, built on the Arroyo Seco in 1901. *Courtesy of The Judson Studios.*

authors, artists, and artisans settled near the Arroyo, and two academic institutions built on sites in the area. Occidental College, founded in 1887, moved from its Boyle Heights campus to Highland Park in 1898. (It moved again, in 1914, to its present location in Eagle Rock.) Historian Robert Glass Cleland describes Highland Park in 1898 as "little more than a sparsely settled farming community. The wooded channel of the Arroyo Seco and the steep hills beyond were a virtual wilderness.... In the valley were a few widely separated ranches, two or three newly erected houses in a recently opened residential subdivision, a beer garden and camp meeting ground where Sycamore Grove Park now stands, and almost nothing else." The beauty of the Arroyo delighted the young women at Occidental, who requested permission for lunchtime picnicking in what they called "The Gully."

In 1901 the College of Fine Arts of the University of Southern California opened on Avenue 66 in Highland Park. The college bulletin painted an idyllic picture of the setting: "on a cliff overlooking an unspoiled natural park, the famed Arroyo Seco, with a perennial stream and groves of magnificent trees, rocks, cliffs, and acres of boulders, wide stretches of oak-dotted sward, and the snow-capped mountains closing every vista."

Artist William Lees Judson, who had settled by the Arroyo in 1893, was founding dean of the College of Fine Arts. He also was founding president of the Arroyo Guild, "an association of expert workers who design and make beautiful things." Inspired by William Morris and Gustav Stickley ("the American William Morris"), the Guild brought to the Arroyo a local version of the Arts

The first and only issue of the *Arroyo Craftsman*.

and Crafts movement. George Wharton James, at one time associate editor of Stickley's *Craftsman* magazine, edited the one and only issue of the Guild's own publication, the *Arroyo Craftsman*. Launched in October 1909, the short-lived journal was intended as "a quarterly magazine of simple living, high thinking, pure democracy, genuine art, honest craftsmanship, natural inspiration, and exalted aspiration."

The Arroyo Guild maintained headquarters in the second College of Fine Arts building (the first burned down in 1910). Still visible over the entrance to the building is the Guild's crest: a rising sun, a hammer in an artisan's hand, and the motto "We Can"–a variant of mottos associated with both William Morris and Gustav Stickley (and with Jan van Eyck before them). The old Arroyo Guild building, now a Los Angeles Historic-Cultural Monument, has long been home to The Judson Studios, a stained-glass firm started in 1897 in the old Plaza area of Los Angeles by one of Judson's sons.

A leading spirit in what has been termed the Arroyo Culture was Charles Fletcher Lummis, whose distinctive house on the west bank of the Arroyo was a lively gathering place for friends who shared some of his many interests: literature, language, music, art, ethnology, and archaeology–as well as "An Old California Good Time."

Mary Austin, who spent several months by the Arroyo in 1899, often visited the nearby Lummis home. There she found literary encouragement and intellectual stimulus. Lummis published some of Mary Austin's early work: poems, short stories, and a novelette. Another writer whose early work appeared in *Land of Sunshine* was Idah Meacham Strobridge, who moved from

Olive Percival hanging a Japanese lantern for one of her famous garden teas. Miss Percival and her neighbors Idah Strobridge and Charles Lummis were noted for their hospitality to artists, authors and bibliophiles. *Courtesy of Huntington Library.*

Nevada to California in 1901 and built a large bungalow at the edge of the Arroyo, just a few blocks from El Alisal. She named her house "At the Sign of the Sagebrush," and in it she operated her Artemisia Bindery. "A commercial-bound book looks cheap beside her staunch and honest and tasteful bindings," wrote Lummis. The Artemisia Bindery published several books, including three by Mrs. Strobridge. Two have illustrations by Maynard Dixon, an occasional visitor to the Arroyo. In addition to her bindery, Mrs. Strobridge had a gallery in her home. "The Little Corner of Local Art" exhibited the work of local artists and displayed autographed books by local authors.

On the slopes of Mount Washington, above El Alisal, landscape artists Elmer and Marion Wachtel built a Craftsman bungalow-studio in 1906. Elmer Wachtel carved his own furniture and designed and cast the metal hinges and fastenings. *Land of Sunshine* for March 1896 carried an appreciative article on Elmer Wachtel, whose pen-and-ink drawings often appeared in the magazine. His vignettes identified two departments in the magazine: one devoted to the Landmarks Club, and the other to book reviews by Lummis ("That Which Is Written"). It was said of Marion Wachtel that she could paint from memory any native tree or shrub that she had ever seen. The Wachtel Home, on West Avenue 43, is a Los Angeles Historic-Cultural Monument.

Numerous authors, artists, bibliophiles, and flower lovers visited the two-story, half-timbered house built by Olive Percival on San Pascual Avenue in 1899. To her diary she confided: "My `dream' house is beautiful; everything in it is beautiful in the truest sense; the man-

The Abbey San Encino, built near the Arroyo by printer Clyde Browne. *Photograph by Charles Puck. Courtesy of Huntington Library.*

agement of it is intelligent; and all who enter are soothed and inspired. William Morris would know what I mean." She planted a series of gardens on her Arroyo acre and filled her home (which she called "The Down-hyl Claim") with remarkable collections of books, dolls, daguerreotypes, pewter, silver, Lalique, and Oriental art. Her garden teas and moon-viewing parties were notable events. An artist at heart (an insurance clerk by profession), she made clever designs with scissors and paper; took interesting photographs (some appeared in *Land of Sunshine*, some in *House Beautiful*); and wrote poetry, short stories, and travel literature.

Not far from the Down-hyl Claim, on Arroyo Glen Street, printer Clyde Browne built his Abbey San Encino. Combining elements of California mission and medieval castle, the Abbey has cloisters, a belltower, chapel, minstrel gallery, and dungeon. Browne worked on the building from 1915 to 1929. Stones from the Arroyo were his chief building material; but he also used brick, tile, and railroad ties, and he incorporated fragments gathered from various historic sites. He also fashioned sheet metal from old automobile bodies into ornaments for the chapel.

The west wing of the Abbey housed the press and bindery. For thirty years Browne did printing for Occidental College, and he maintained close ties with faculty and students. Browne also printed work that he himself had written: poems, a play, a book on the missions, and several booklets about construction of the Abbey. The medievalism of some of Browne's typography shows the influence of William Morris and of Elbert Hubbard's Roycroft Press.

Drawing by Ernest Batchelder of his Pasadena residence on the east bank of the Arroyo. *Courtesy of Robert W. Winter.*

Alongside the Abbey San Encino, Browne built a series of little stone studios for what he hoped would become a community of artisans. Two young Occidental graduates, Ward Ritchie and Lawrence Clark Powell, rented one of the studios in 1929. Powell learned to play the chapel organ, and Ritchie used the press equipment on Sundays upon the payment of a dollar. Abbey San Encino, which is still owned and occupied by the Browne family, is a Los Angeles Historic-Cultural Monument.

Gustav Stickley's *Craftsman* magazine inspired the name of the American Arts and Crafts movement and popularized "the simple but artistic bungalow." As described by Stickley, "The house, the garden, the terrace, the patio, the open porch are all one domain, one shelter from the outside world. It is home in that big, fine sense of the word that leaves the horizon, not four walls, for the boundary lines." Pasadena naturalist Charles Francis Saunders gave a more precise definition. "When you see a cozy one or one-and-a-half storied dwelling," he wrote, "with low-pitched roof and very wide eaves, ample porches, lots of windows and an outside chimney of cobble or clinker-brick half hidden by clinging vines–that is a bungalow."

The May 1915 issue of the *Craftsman* featured the Pasadena bungalow that Ernest A. Batchelder built in 1909 on South Arroyo Boulevard, at the east rim of the Arroyo Seco. A master tilemaker, Batchelder had strong ties to the Arts and Crafts movement. He had studied in England at the Birmingham School of Arts and Crafts; taught design theory and manual arts at the Minneapolis Guild of Handicrafts, which he helped found; and served as director of art at Pasadena's Throop Polytechnic

Jean Mannheim's Arroyo studio, with some of his paintings displayed. *Photograph by David Brandt. Courtesy of Ann Scheid.*

Institute (forerunner of Caltech), which emphasized "true culture of head, hand, and heart." Batchelder wrote many articles for the *Craftsman*, and he published two influential books on design. His own house, which he designed in Swiss Chalet style, is on the National Register of Historic Places.

At the rear of his property, Batchelder built a small studio, set up a kiln, and began producing his famous decorative tiles. The Batchelder house incorporates some of the tiles in walls and floors and in a magnificent fireplace. One of the fireplace tiles shows a sketching rabbit, which was Batchelder's crest. Another tile depicts a harp: the crest of his wife, Alice Coleman Batchelder. A pianist and organist, in 1904 she founded the Coleman Chamber Music Association, the oldest continuing chamber music association in the country.

Not far from the Batchelder house is the shingled bungalow that the artist Jean Mannheim built in 1909 as a residence, studio, and gallery. Mannheim was greatly admired for his portraits (including one of naturalist John Burroughs) and for landscapes that show a lyrical sense of light and color. He was an authority on fine bindings, having learned the art of bookbinding as a young man in Germany, and he was also a violinist and an enthusiastic gardener. Mannheim considered the Arroyo an artist's paradise because he had only to step outside to find subjects to paint. A prolific artist, his landscapes are said to have brought bits of Pasadena into homes across the country.

"Among those who have helped make the homes of California proverbial for wise planning and structural beauty," said a *Craftsman* article in 1912, "perhaps none has contributed more effectively than the well-known

MUSEUMS ALONG THE ARROYO

The majestic Arroyo boulder fireplace in the Hindry Residence.
Charles Greene made the original drawings for the fireplace.
Photograph by Tom M. Apostol.

Pasadena firm of Greene & Greene." Along the east bank of the Upper Arroyo is an extraordinary collection of homes designed by Charles and Henry Greene. Chief among them is the elegant Gamble House, "the ultimate bungalow" and a National Historic Landmark.

Some of the other noted architects represented in the area are Robert F. Farquhar, Arthur and Alfred Heineman, Myron Hunt, and Frank Lloyd Wright. Farquhar designed the imposing Fenyes Mansion, an example of the grand homes built at the turn of the century on Orange Grove Avenue, once known as Millionaires' Row. The Fenyes Mansion, located at Walnut and Orange Grove, is now the home of the Pasadena Historical Museum.

On Prospect Boulevard, a short walk from the Gamble House, is the spacious home designed by the Heineman brothers for mining engineer Willis Hindry and his wife Mary. The mansion incorporates numerous Craftsman elements, including sensitive use of wood and a magnificent Arroyo boulder fireplace. Much of the design of the house is credited to Alfred Heineman, a former student of Ernest Batchelder. Indeed, said Heineman, his only formal art education was the design class that Batchelder taught at Throop Polytechnic Institute.

The Hindry House is just one of many landmark houses built along the Arroyo in the Prospect Historic District, an entire Pasadena neighborhood listed in the National Register of Historic Places. On Prospect Crescent is La Miniatura, the house designed by Frank Lloyd Wright for Alice Millard, a bibliophile and dealer in rare books. "I would rather have built this little house than St. Peter's in Rome," Wright is quoted as saying. He not only designed the house, the first of his "textile-block" constructions,

La Miniatura, designed by Frank Lloyd Wright for Pasadena bibliophile Alice Millard. The house, built in 1923, is the earliest example of Wright's "textile-block" construction. *Photograph by Patricia Adler-Ingram. Courtesy of Huntington Library.*

but he chose the site, on a small ravine that emptied into the Arroyo Seco. Like a number of other Arroyo residents (including Olive Percival, William Lees Judson, Clyde Browne, and Ernest Batchelder), Alice Millard was a great admirer of William Morris. In 1929, to aid the William Morris Memorial Fund, she arranged an exhibit at La Miniatura of fifty-three books printed by Morris at his Kelmscott Press.

Myron Hunt, who designed a Craftsman house by the Arroyo for his family, also designed the most visible landmark in the Arroyo Seco: Pasadena's Rose Bowl. It was built in 1922 on a site being used as a dump. The area was transformed by 16,000 rose bushes planted on slopes of the fill to control erosion. Because of lack of money, several features of Hunt's original plan for the stadium were abandoned, including a facade of neoclassic arches and eight buffalo statues at the portals.

Hunt designed a more modest structure on the east bank of Pasadena's Lower Arroyo Seco. The building is La Casita del Arroyo, a little stone clubhouse near the Colorado Street Bridge, a Civil Engineering Landmark whose nine graceful arches span the Arroyo Seco. La Casita, dedicated in 1933, served two purposes: to employ the jobless and to provide a community meeting place for Pasadena citizens. La Casita was a joint project of the Pasadena Garden Club and the Pasadena Park Department. Architect Myron Hunt donated the building plans and supervised construction without charge. Almost no building material had to be purchased. The walls are Arroyo boulders, the original roof shakes were cut from fallen trees, and most of the lumber was salvaged from the bicycle track built in the Rose Bowl for the 1932 Olympics. The building was restored in 1987,

MUSEUMS ALONG THE ARROYO

Early scene in the Arroyo Seco. *Courtesy of the Archives at the Pasadena Historical Museum.*

after suffering fire damage, and the landscaping was redesigned. Both projects involved the active cooperation of the Pasadena Garden Club and the City of Pasadena. Landscape architects Yoshiro Befu and Isabelle Greene (granddaughter of architect Henry Greene) designed three demonstration areas, including a "super water-saver" garden. Plantings alongside the entrance re-create a landscaping style common to Southern California gardens in the first half of the century. From La Casita a path leads down to a pleasant hiking trail through the Arroyo.

Pasadena has declared the Lower Arroyo Seco, from the Colorado Street Bridge to the South Pasadena border, a historic landmark. Efforts are underway to restore to its natural state a small area between the Colorado Street and La Loma Street bridges. The city's long-range plan calls for planting native trees, shrubs, and wildflowers in the area, and for creating a low-flow stream by diverting water from the concrete channel. Attention is being focused also on the Upper Arroyo Seco. Volunteers have planted hundreds of oaks and other indigenous trees north of Devil's Gate Dam in an area being developed as the Hahamongna Watershed Park. One of the numerous villages established centuries ago by the Gabrielino people inspired the park's name of Hahamongna. The word translates as "flowing waters, fruitful valley."

The Arroyo continues to attract artists, authors, nature lovers, and admirers of good architecture. An article published in Stickley's *Craftsman* magazine in 1912 sums up what friends of the Arroyo are determined to preserve: "Nature with all her kindness, simplicity, quiet and restfulness."

Facing page: Entrance to the Fenyes Mansion.
Photograph by Tom M. Apostol.

Pasadena Historical Museum

On a January afternoon in 1874, the first Pasadena colonists gathered to select homesites along the Arroyo Seco. They met on Reservoir Hill, a vanished landmark that was not far from the present site of the Pasadena Historical Museum. The museum is located at the corner of Orange Grove Boulevard and Walnut Street, on the grounds of an estate once owned by Adalbert and Eva Scott Fenyes.

Since its founding in 1924, the museum has pursued the goal set by its first president: "To collect data from our past and to preserve and collect that which will be made today and in the days to come." For a few years one filing cabinet held the museum's entire historical collection. Today the research library and archives occupy one floor in the museum's new History Center building. Upon completion the History Center also will contain an education hall, exhibit hall, and conference room, as well as a new and enlarged gift store.

A photograph from the museum's vast collection documenting Pasadena history. This is the Hotel Green dining room, Christmas 1896. *Courtesy of the Archives at the Pasadena Historical Museum.*

PASADENA HISTORICAL MUSEUM

The Pasadena Historical Museum has an unparalleled collection of material relating to the San Gabriel Valley. Among its holdings are nearly a million photographs of Pasadena and the surrounding area, several thousand reference works on Pasadena and Southern California, more than 450 personal scrapbooks, an extensive collection of maps dating from the 19th century, and a wide range of ephemera dating from the 1870s to the present. (One interesting early item is an 1895 Crown City Cycle Club stock certificate.) The museum's special collections include the Pasadena Olympic Stars collection, the Tournament of Roses collection, and the Black History collection. The museum also owns a costume and textile collection that contains 2,500 pieces.

The museum offers numerous programs to the community. These include changing exhibits on local history, guided tours of the historic Fenyes Mansion, art exhibits, musical programs, educational lectures and seminars, and tours and special programs for schoolchildren. The museum is committed to presenting programs that represent the diverse cultural background of Pasadena's citizens, past and present. "The Pasadena Historical Museum is the community's only museum and educational facility devoted solely to our local history and culture," says executive director Jane Auerbach.

The Pasadena Historical Museum fondly refers to the turn-of-the-century Fenyes Mansion on the property as its largest artifact. Robert D. Farquhar designed the house in 1905 for Adalbert and Eva Scott Fenyes. It is Beaux Arts in style, with Classical Revival elements. A two-story addition, designed by Sylvanus Marston, was

Eva Scott Fenyes, Leonora Muse Curtin, Leonora Curtin, and Adalbert Fenyes photographed outside the family mansion. *Courtesy of the Archives at the Pasadena Historical Museum.*

built on the north side of the house in 1911. For nearly one hundred years the Fenyes Mansion has played a significant role in Pasadena's cultural life. It has been a gathering place for artists, authors, scientists, and musicians; has served as the first Finnish Consulate in Southern California; and since 1970 has been preserved as a historical museum. Docents lead tours of the mansion, which is one of the few remaining examples of the great houses built along fashionable Orange Grove Avenue early in the century.

Adalbert and Eva Scott Fenyes moved to Pasadena in 1896 shortly after their marriage in Dr. Fenyes's native Hungary. Pasadena was a flourishing city in 1896, renowned for its climate and its cultural environment. The city had a Grand Opera House, a public library with more than 10,000 volumes, and a new polytechnic institute, the forerunner of Caltech. Pasadena also had electric trolleys, 24-hour telephone service, an annual Tournament of Roses parade, and the famous Mount Lowe "Railway in the Clouds."

Dr. Fenyes was a physician and surgeon, a pioneer in the medical use of X-rays. He was also a noted entomologist and published a profusely illustrated two-volume work on insects. Following his death his collections and library were deposited in the Academy of Sciences in Golden Gate Park. Eva Scott Fenyes was an accomplished artist. She recorded her travels, which spanned three continents, in hundreds of sketches and watercolor paintings. Fifteen albums with her watercolors are preserved in the archives of the History Center. At the suggestion of Charles Fletcher Lummis, founder of the Landmarks Club, she also made watercolor paintings of

MUSEUMS ALONG THE ARROYO

The Fenyes Mansion studio. It was the setting for art exhibits, concerts, plays, and Friday afternoon at-homes. *Courtesy of the Archives at the Pasadena Historical Museum.*

the old adobes, missions, and other historic buildings of California. Over a period of more than thirty years she made 301 paintings of significant early buildings located between San Diego and Sonoma. She bequeathed those paintings to the Southwest Museum. Many of her other paintings can be seen in the Fenyes Mansion.

The 1911 addition to the house provided office and laboratory space on the ground floor for Dr. Fenyes, and a solarium and studio above. The solarium was used as a greenhouse for ferns and orchids. It also provided an unusual setting for parties. On such occasions a huge board was placed over the stairwell opening to serve as a buffet table.

Mrs. Fenyes did her painting in the studio, and displayed paintings by other artists there. The studio was the setting also for Friday afternoon at-homes, for Spanish and Italian classes, and for plays and concerts. Actors could make their entrances and exits by way of a trap door and a spiral staircase leading to Dr. Fenyes's downstairs office. Musicians performed on the studio's stairway balcony.

The Fenyes Mansion richly suggests the way of life enjoyed by wealthy, cultured Pasadenans of the early twentieth century. There are Oriental rugs throughout the house, silk damask wall coverings in the living room, and a 17th century Flemish tapestry in the grand entry hall. Nearly every room contains antique pieces. Among them are a 17th century carved wooden chest, an 18th century long-case clock, and a 19th century Victorian sofa. One interesting piece is a drop-front desk, or vargueno, made in Spain in the 16th century. The interior has secret compartments and ornamentation in gilded bone and ivory.

MUSEUMS ALONG THE ARROYO

The Fenyes Mansion in 1918, the backdrop for a motion picture starring cowboy actor Tom Mix. *Courtesy of the Archives at the Pasadena Historical Museum.*

Only one piece of furniture was not in the house when the family lived there. It is a tall grandfather's clock with a mechanism that rotates colored glass slides of early Pasadena. A gift to the Pasadena Historical Museum, the clock originally belonged to the luxurious Raymond Hotel, which dominated a hill just south of the Pasadena border.

Paintings by noted artists hang throughout the Fenyes Mansion. Among the artists represented are William Keith, William Merritt Chase, Carl Oscar Borg, Granville Redmond, Benjamin Brown, and Charles Walter Stetson. One William Keith landscape includes the figure of his friend Eva Scott Fenyes. Objets d'art in the house include a Baroque reliquary, a signed Tiffany lamp, and a tortoise shell tea caddy.

Family members other than Adalbert and Eva Scott Fenyes lived in the mansion at various times. They were Leonora Muse Curtin (Mrs. Fenyes's daughter by a previous marriage); Mrs. Curtin's daughter (another Leonora), who married Y. A. Paloheimo of Finland; and the four Paloheimo children. The two Leonoras, like Eva Scott Fenyes, were noted patrons of the arts. In Santa Fe they helped establish markets for the traditional crafts produced by weavers, woodcarvers, and other artisans in the old Hispanic villages of New Mexico. Leonora Muse Curtin is known also as the author of two books based on her study of native plants of the Southwest used for food, flavoring, and medicine. *Healing Herbs of the Upper Rio Grande,* with an introduction by her friend Mary Austin, was first published in Santa Fe, then reprinted by the Southwest Museum.

In 1946 Y. A. Paloheimo–husband of the second

The Finnish Folk Art Museum, displaying handmade utensils, furniture, and crafts from various provinces of Finland.
Courtesy of the Archives at the Pasadena Historical Museum.

Leonora–was appointed Finnish consul in the Southwestern United States, and from 1946 to 1965 the Fenyes Mansion served as the Finnish Consulate. In 1949 Consul Paloheimo moved a little redwood building to the property for use as a guesthouse. A Swiss-chalet style structure, designed in 1910 by Frederick Roehrig, the building originally was a garage on the South Orange Grove estate of lumber tycoon Arthur H. Fleming. The building is now the home of the Finnish Folk Art Museum. It contains a sauna room, a large living room with an open hearth, and a room displaying farmhouse furnishings. It is the only such exhibit outside of Finland, and is cosponsored by the Pasadena Historical Museum and the Finlandia Foundation, established by Y. A. Paloheimo in 1953.

In 1965, when the children of the fourth generation were grown, the Curtin-Paloheimo family selected the Pasadena Historical Society (now called the Pasadena Historical Museum) as the recipient of the Fenyes home and garden. The dedication ceremony, with family members present, was held on June 11, 1970. The Fenyes Mansion is a Pasadena Cultural Heritage Landmark and is on the National Register of Historic Places.

Facing page: Entrance to the Gamble House.
Photograph by Tom M . Apostol.

The Gamble House

The David B. Gamble House in Pasadena is the masterpiece of architects Charles and Henry Greene and an elegant expression of the American Arts and Crafts movement. The Greenes absorbed the craftsman aesthetic as students in St. Louis at the pioneering Manual Training High School, whose motto was "The Cultured Mind, The Skillful Hand." After graduating from high school the brothers studied architecture at the Massachusetts Institute of Technology, then worked from 1891 until 1893 in Boston architectural firms.

In 1893 the Greenes traveled to Pasadena for a visit with their parents, and en route stopped in Chicago to see the World's Columbian Exposition. The architecture, craftsmanship, and landscaping of the Japanese Pavilion inspired elements of their own later work. Once arrived in Pasadena, the brothers decided to remain, and they opened an office on Colorado Street, near Fair Oaks Avenue. Replying to a questionnaire from Charles

MUSEUMS ALONG THE ARROYO

The Gamble House under construction in 1908. In front of the house are Mary and David Gamble with Henry M. Greene. Clarence Gamble is standing on the upper sleeping porch. His brother, Sidney Gamble, took the photograph. *Courtesy of Greene and Greene Library.*

Lummis for the history files of the Los Angeles Public Library, Charles Greene wrote that the brothers had a three-fold objective as architects: "1st to understand as many phases of Human Life as possible. 2nd to provide for its individual requirements in the most practical and useful way. 3rd to make these necessary and useful things pleasurable."

While the Greenes were establishing their reputation as architects in the early 1890s, David Berry Gamble was helping run the Cincinnati-based Procter & Gamble Company, of which his father was a founding partner. Like many wealthy Midwesterners at the turn of the century, David and Mary Gamble spent their winters in the Pasadena area, staying at great resort hotels like the Raymond. In 1907 they decided to build a home in Pasadena and bought property on Westmoreland Place, a private street with wonderful views of the Arroyo Seco and the San Gabriel Mountains. As their architects, the Gambles chose Charles and Henry Greene, who had designed a dozen houses in the neighborhood, including one on Westmoreland Place. The *Craftsman* magazine for July 1907 featured Charles Greene's own home, on nearby Arroyo Terrace.

Work on the Gamble House began in March 1908 and was completed the following January, a month ahead of schedule. Although three stories high and 8,100 square feet in area, the house has a long, low profile. Its horizontal lines are emphasized by the broad terraces and cantilevered sleeping porches and by the dramatic roof overhang, with exposed beams and projecting rafters. The overhanging eaves did more than merely shade the house. "As the day progressed," observed Randell

MUSEUMS ALONG THE ARROYO

The dramatic entry hall of the Gamble House. *Photograph by Maynard Parker. Courtesy of Greene and Greene Library.*

Makinson in one of his many appreciative studies of the Gamble House, "shadows from the rafter ends projecting beyond the edge of the rolled roof danced across the structure. Consequently, the house appeared to be constantly alive and changing."

The Gamble House has been called a symphony in wood. The exterior is clad in split redwood shakes stained a soft green to blend into the landscape. The interior makes sensitive use of redwood, teak, mahogany, maple, oak, and Port Orford cedar. Each element is lovingly sculpted and hand-rubbed to a lustrous finish. Japanese-inspired joinery contributes to the overall design. "The whole construction was carefully thought out, and there was a reason for every detail," Henry Greene once said of the brothers' work. "The idea was to eliminate everything unnecessary to make the whole as direct and simple as possible, but always with the beautiful in mind as the final goal." To help achieve the excellence they demanded, the Greenes relied on highly skilled workers, and in particular on two superb craftsmen: cabinetmaker John Hall and stair builder Peter Hall, who also served as the building contractor.

Edward Bosley, director of the Gamble House, has called its entry hall "among the most moving domestic spaces in America." The great front door is a stunning work of art. Flowing across its three panels and three transoms is the design of a magnificent California live oak. The design was conceived by Charles Greene (who had a similar tree on his own property) and was executed in leaded art glass by Los Angeles master craftsman Emil Lange. Just inside the teak-paneled hall is a beautifully crafted staircase. Its handrails have a sensuous quality

The Gamble House living room. Structure and furnishings blend into one harmonious composition. *Photograph by Leroy Hulbert. Courtesy of Greene and Greene Library.*

that invites the touch. At the far end of the hall are double doors that look out on the rear terrace and the little fishpond with its undulating wall of clinker bricks. The Oriental "cloud-lift" motif on the terrace doors is echoed on windows and furniture throughout the house.

The Greenes believed in total design, a harmonious union of landscape, house, and furnishings. "In a work of art as in a piece of tapestry," Charles Greene explained, "the same thread runs through the web, but goes to make up different figures." He designed most of the furnishings in the Gamble House–from carpets to chandeliers, from light switch plates to fireplace tools, from tables and chairs to an upright piano. For the study, however, the specially designed furniture was never built. David Gamble preferred using pieces he had brought from Cincinnati, including his Morris chair and roll-top desk. A large fireplace of pressed brick dominates the little room. The craftsman's touch is apparent in the hand-rounded bricks used at the fireplace opening.

A door across the hall from the study leads to the guest wing, which contains a bedroom, divided bathroom, and walk-in closet. As in most other rooms of the house, subtle details suggest the outdoors. The design of a rose appears in the art-glass wall sconces and at the head and foot of the two nickel silver beds. Except for the beds, the furniture is bird's-eye maple, with inlays of silver wire and Indonesian vermillion wood.

At the heart of the Gamble House is the spacious teak-paneled living room, an open and inviting space with distinct areas for books, for music, and for inglenook seating by the fireplace. Five rugs woven from Charles Greene's watercolor designs add subtle color to the

The Gamble House dining room. Every element relates to the total design. *Photograph by Leroy Hulbert. Courtesy of Greene and Greene Library.*

room. Color is introduced also by art-glass panels in the cabinet doors; opalescent, leaded-glass lighting fixtures; and an iridescent glass mosaic of a vine that trails across the Grueby tile fireplace. Encircling the room is a carved redwood frieze with images of clouds, trees, and birds. An alcove opposite from the fireplace looks out on terrace, garden, and arroyo.

The dining room also looks out on garden and terrace, while a suggestion of nature is brought indoors by leaded art-glass windows that suggest flowering roses. (Roses grow just beyond the window, and the Gambles' coat-of-arms depicts a crane and a rose.) The dining room is in mahogany: its most dramatic feature a built-in sideboard and a beautifully sculptured and ingeniously engineered table that can extend to seat fourteen, while the pedestal remains stationary. Above the table (and echoing its shape) is a large leaded-glass chandelier framed in mahogany and suspended by leather straps. A Tiffany fern bowl in Mrs. Gamble's collection inspired the flowing design on the Grueby tile fireplace.

The large service area adjoining the dining room reveals the same thoughtful planning and attention to detail as the other areas of the house. A specially designed cabinet in the butler's pantry has slots for the dining room table leaves. Extra-wide drawers permit the storage of tablecloths on rollers. The maple work table, with its double-ended drawers, provides a convenient service island in the kitchen. Just outside the kitchen is a porch used as a dining area by the housekeeper and the cook.

From the splendid central hall of the Gamble House, the sculptural teak staircase leads to the family's living

The rear patio of the Gamble House, with the two great eucalyptus trees that once grew there. *Photograph by Leroy Hulbert. Courtesy of Greene and Greene Library.*

quarters. The second-floor rooms, which are pleasantly informal, include the master bedroom (more than twenty feet square), a suite for Mary Gamble's maiden sister Julia Huggins, and a sitting room/study for the two younger Gamble sons. (They slept outdoors on their own "covered balcony.") The master bedroom and the suite for Miss Huggins ("Aunt Julia") also had their own sleeping porch. Aunt Julia's porch looks down on the rear terrace and on the fishpond, in which stepping stones protrude from the water like little islands.

Aunt Julia brought her own brass bed with her from Cincinnati. Charles Greene designed other pieces for the bedroom in ash and woven rattan. For the two teenage boys, the Greenes chose oak furniture made in Gustav Stickley's Craftsman Workshops. Furniture in the master bedroom is black walnut, with delicate inlays in floral designs inspired by two of Mary Gamble's Rookwood vases.

The third floor space (24 by 29 feet) followed the design of a billiard room planned for another Greene and Greene house. Billiards did not interest David Gamble, however, and the upstairs room was used for storage. The room is paneled in Douglas fir and Port Orford cedar and is ringed with windows. These afford wonderful views and also contribute to effective air circulation throughout the house. Architectural historian Reyner Banham has admiringly compared the room to the cabin of a wooden ship.

David Gamble died in 1923, Mary Gamble in 1929, and her sister, Julia Huggins, in 1943. The Gambles' oldest son, Cecil, and his wife Louise considered selling the family home after Aunt Julia's death. They quickly aban-

An early photograph of the Gamble House.
Courtesy of Greene and Greene Library.

doned the idea, however, when the prospective buyers mentioned their desire to cover the natural hand-rubbed wood surfaces with white paint. Aware of the architectural significance of their home, Cecil and Louise Gamble opened it to interested visitors, including the design faculty and students at the University of Southern California School of Architecture.

In 1966 the heirs of Cecil and Louise Gamble presented the Gamble House and its original furnishings to the City of Pasadena in a joint agreement with the University of Southern California. Another valuable gift came from the children and grandchildren of Charles and Henry Greene, who contributed drawings, photographs, letters, and other documents to the Gamble House collection. On October 12, 1968, the hundredth anniversary of Charles Sumner Greene's birth, the Gamble House dedicated the Greene and Greene Library, an archival resource for the study of Charles and Henry Greene, their contemporaries, and the Arts and Crafts movement. The Gamble House Greene and Greene Library is housed in the Virginia Steele Scott Gallery of the Huntington Library. The Gamble House Bookstore is located in the former garage on the Westmoreland property.

In 1952 the American Institute of Architects honored Charles and Henry Greene as great creative Americans, "formulators of a new and native architecture." The Gamble House is the best-preserved example of their work and the most complete embodiment of their design philosophy. Discussing the legacy of the Gamble House, Edward Bosley has said, "It represents no social or political ideology, nor a manifesto of design, but gives a glimpse at the pure love of architecture, as felt and

Charles Sumner Greene and
Henry Mather Greene in
1908. *Courtesy of Greene and
Greene Library.*

expressed by two men who thought less about proclaiming influence on the profession than they cared about the union of art and craft."

Museum Information

Because hours and admission fees are subject to change, visitors are advised to call the individual museums for any updated information, including holiday schedules and information on special programs.

El Alisal: The Lummis Home

Address: 200 East Avenue 43, Highland Park
(Avenue 43 exit off the 110 Freeway)
Telephone: (213) 222-0546
Hours: Friday-Sunday, 12:00 p.m. to 4:00 p.m.
Admission: Free

The Gamble House

Address: 4 Westmoreland Place, Pasadena
(One-quarter mile north of Colorado Boulevard. Enter from 300 block of North Orange Grove Boulevard.)
Telephone: (818) 793-3334 or (213) 681-6427
Hours: Thursday-Sunday, 12:00 p.m. to 3:00 p.m.
Admission: Adults $5.00, seniors $4.00, students $3.00, members and children 12 and under free

The Gamble House Greene and Greene Library is housed in the Virginia Steele Scott Gallery of the Huntington Library at 1151 Oxford Road, San Marino. The library is open Tuesdays and Thursdays, 1:00 p.m. to 4 p.m. Appointments can be made by calling (818) 405-2232.

MUSEUMS ALONG THE ARROYO

HERITAGE SQUARE MUSEUM

Address: 3800 Homer Street, Highland Park
(Avenue 43 exit off the 110 Freeway)
Telephone:(818) 449-0193
Hours: Friday, 10:00 a.m. to 3:00 p.m.; Saturdays, Sundays, and holiday Mondays, 11:30 a.m. to 4:30 p.m.
Admission: adults $5.00, seniors and juniors $4.00, youths (7-11) $2.00, members and children 6 and under free

---

PASADENA HISTORICAL MUSEUM

Address: 470 West Walnut Street, Pasadena
(at North Orange Grove Boulevard)
Telephone: (818) 577-1660
Tour hours: Thursday-Sunday, 1:00 p.m. to 4 p.m.
Admission: Adults $4.00, seniors and students $3.00, members and children under 12 free
The Research Center of the Pasadena Historical Museum is open Thursday-Sunday, 1:00 p.m. to 4:00 p.m. For an appointment call (818) 577-1660.

SOUTHWEST MUSEUM

Address: Corner of Marmion Way and Museum Drive, Los Angeles
(Avenue 43 exit off the 110 Freeway)
Telephone: (213) 221-2164, ext. 221
Hours: Tuesday-Sunday, 11:00 a.m. to 5:00 p.m.
Admission: Adults $5.00, seniors and students $3.00, youths (7-18) $2.00, members and children 6 and under free
The Braun Research Library of the Southwest Museum is open to the public Wednesday-Saturday, 1:00 p.m. to 5:00 p.m.

Selected Reading List

THE SUNNY SEVENTIES AND BOOMING EIGHTIES

Baur, John E. *Health Seekers of Southern California.* San Marino: Huntington Library, 1959.

Bixby Smith, Sarah. *Adobe Days.* Cedar Rapids: The Torch Press, 1926.

Dumke, Glenn S. *The Boom of the Eighties in Southern California.* San Marino: Huntington Library, 1944.

Guinn, J. M. "The Great Real Estate Boom of 1887." *Historical Society of Southern California Annual Publication* 1 (1890): 13-21.

Hylen, Arnold. *Los Angeles Before the Freeways, 1850-1950. Images of an Era.* Los Angeles: Dawson's Book Shop, 1981.

Illustrated History of Los Angeles County, California. Chicago: Lewis Publishing Company, 1889.

Netz, Joseph. "The Great Los Angeles Real Estate Boom of 1887." *Historical Society of Southern California Annual Publication* 10 (1915-16): 64-68.

Newmark, Maurice H., and Marco R. Newmark, eds. *Sixty Years in Southern California, 1853-1913. Containing the Reminiscences of Harris Newmark.* 4th ed. Los Angeles: Zeitlin & Ver Brugge, 1970.

Nordhoff, Charles. *California: For Health, Pleasure, and Residence.* New York: Harper & Bros., 1872.

Raitt, Helen and Mary Collier Wayne, eds. *We Three Came West: A True Chronicle.* San Diego: Tofua Press, 1974.

Salvator, Ludwig Louis. *Los Angeles in the Sunny Seventies: A Golden Blossom from the Golden Land.* Translated by Marguerite Eyer Wilbur. Los Angeles: Bruce McCallister-Jake Zeitlin, 1929.

Truman, Ben C. *Semi-Tropical California: Its Climate,*

Healthfulness, Productiveness, and Scenery. San Francisco: A. L. Bancroft Co., 1874.

Van Dyke, Theodore S. *Millionaires of a Day: An Inside Story of the Great Southern California 'Boom.'* New York: Fords, Howard & Hulbert, 1890.

Wilson, John Albert. *History of Los Angeles County California.* Oakland: Thompson and West, 1880.

THE LUMMIS HOUSE

Apostol, Jane. *El Alisal: Where History Lingers.* Los Angeles: Historical Society of Southern California, 1994.

Fiske, Turbesé Lummis and Keith Lummis. *Charles Fletcher Lummis: The Man and His West.* Norman: University of Oklahoma, 1975.

THE SOUTHWEST MUSEUM

Masterkey 61 (Summer/Fall 1987): 1-48.

Moneta, Daniela, ed. *Chas. F. Lummis: The Centennial Exhibition. Commemorating His Tramp Across the Continent.* Los Angeles: Southwest Museum, 1985.

Robinson, W. W. *The Story of the Southwest Museum.* Los Angeles, Ward Ritchie Press, 1960.

Selmer, Doris and Jerome Selmer. *The First Museum in Los Angeles.* Arcadia (California), 1993. [Limited edition miniature book.]

THE ARROYO SECO

Andersen, Timothy, Eudorah M. Moore, and Robert W. Winter, eds. *California Design* 1910. Santa Barbara and Salt Lake City: Peregrine Smith, Inc., 1980.

Apostol, Jane. "Margaret Collier Graham: First Lady of the Foothills." *Southern California Quarterly* 63 (1981): 348-373.

_____.*Olive Percival: Los Angeles Author and Bibliophile.* Los Angeles: University of California (Department of Special Collections, University Research Library), 1992.

Arroyo Craftsman 1 (October 1909).

SELECTED READING LIST

Davies, D. W. *Clyde Browne: His Abbey & His Press*. Pasadena: The Castle Press, 1982.

Goodwin, H. Marshall, Jr. "The Arroyo Seco: From Dry Gulch to Freeway. *Southern California Quarterly* 47 (1965): 73-102.

Sanders, Barry, ed. *The Craftsman: An Anthology*. Santa Barbara: Peregrine Smith, 1978.

Starr, Kevin. *Inventing the Dream. California Through the Progressive Era*. New York and Oxford: Oxford University Press, 1985.

Trapp, Kenneth R., ed. *The Arts and Crafts Movement in California: Living the Good Life*. New York: Abbeville Press, 1993.

Winter, Robert. *The California Bungalow*. Los Angeles: Hennessy & Ingalls, 1980.

Pasadena Historical Museum

Fenyes, Eva Scott, with descriptive text by Isabel López de Fáges. *Thirty-Two Adobe Houses of Old California*. Los Angeles: Southwest Museum, 1950.

Kostlan, Jane and Robert Winter. *The Fenyes Mansion: A Pasadena Cultural Heritage Landmark*. Pasadena: Pasadena Historical Society [1982?].

The Gamble House

Bosley, Edward R. *Gamble House: Greene and Greene*. London: Phaidon Press, 1992.

Makinson, Randell L. *Greene & Greene: Architecture as a Fine Art*. Salt Lake City and Santa Barbara: Peregrine Smith, 1977.

———. *Greene & Greene. Furniture and Related Designs*. Salt Lake City: Gibbs M. Smith, 1982.

———. "Greene and Greene: The Gamble House" and "An Academic Paper: The Gamble House," *Prairie School Review* 5, no. 4 (1968): 5-26.

Thomas, Jeanette A. *Images of the Gamble House: Masterwork of Greene & Greene*. Pasadena: The Gamble House, University of Southern California, 1989.

Index

Abbey San Encino, 91, 93
Alcade Mayor, 61
Andrews, Thomas F., 65
Archaeological Institute of America, 67
Arroyo Craftsman, 87
Arroyo Guild, 85, 87
Arroyo Seco, 17, 23, 81-101, 103
Artemisia Bindery, 89
Arts and Crafts Movement, 85, 87, 93, 115, 127
Auerbach, Jane, 105
Austin, Mary, 83, 87, 111

Baker, Arcadia Bandini Stearns, 21
Baker, Robert, 21
Baker Block, 21
Bandelier, Adolph, 55
Banham, Reyner, 125
Batchelder, Alice Coleman, 95
Batchelder, Ernest, 93, 95, 97, 99
Befu, Yoshiro, 101
Bel Air Garden Club, 37
Benshoff, Will A., 43
Binder, Erwin, 77
Boom of the 80s, 23, 25
Borein, Ed, 53
Bosley, Edward R., 119, 127
Braun, C. Allan, 77
Braun Research Library, 75, 77
Browne, Clyde, 91, 93, 99

California: For Health, Pleasure, and Residence, 19
Carr, Harry, 59
Carriage Barn, 37
Casa de Adobe, 77, 79
Cleland, Robert Glass, 85
Coleman Chamber Music Association, 95

College of Fine Arts, 85, 87
Collier, Jennie, 19
Colonial Dames of America, 33
Colonial Drug, 45
Costansó, Miguel, 81
Craftsman, 93, 95, 101, 117
Crocker, Charles F., 13
Cultural Heritage Foundation of Southern California, 29, 31
Curtin, Leonora Muse, 111
Curtis, Edward S., 77

Dentzel, Carl S., 77
Dixon, Lillian, 53
Dixon, Maynard, 53, 57, 89
Down-hyl Claim, 91

Eagle Rock High School, 37
Eisen, Theodore, 79
El Alisal, 23, 47-65, 71
El Pueblo de Los Angeles State Historic Monument, 15
Ethnobotanical Garden, 71

Farquhar, Robert D., 97, 105
Fenyes, Adalbert, 103, 105, 107, 109
Fenyes, Eva Scott, 103, 105, 107,109, 111, 113
Fenyes Mansion, 97, 105, 107, 111, 113
Finlandia Foundation, 113
Finnish Consulate, 107, 113
Finnish Folk Art Museum, 113
Ford, John J., 41
Ford, William Joseph, 43
Ford (John J.) House, 41, 43
Fowler, Orson S., 39
Frémont, Elizabeth Benton, 69
Frémont, John Charles, 69

Gamble, Cecil, 125, 127

Gamble, David Berry, 117, 121, 125
Gamble, Louise, 125, 127
Gamble, Mary, 117, 123, 125
Gamble House, 97, 115-129
Graham, Margaret Collier, 19
Green, Perry M., 43
Greene, Charles Sumner, 97, 115, 117, 119, 121, 125, 127
Greene, Henry Mather, 97, 101, 115, 117, 119, 121, 125, 127
Greene, Isabelle, 101
Greene and Greene Library, 127

Hahamongna Watershed Park, 101
Hale, Bessie, 35
Hale, James G., 35
Hale House, 33, 35
Hall, John, 119
Hall, Peter, 119
Hamburger, M. A., 69
Hanna, Phil Townsend, 13
Haozous, Bob, 73
Hastings, Walter, 39
Hayes, Benjamin, 17
Healing Herbs of the Upper Rio Grande, 111
Heineman, Alfred, 97
Heineman, Arthur, 97
Herald Pamphlet of 1876, 21
Heritage Square Museum, 17, 27-45, 47
Herlihy, Barry, 33
Hindry House, 97
Hispanic Society of Los Angeles, 79
Historical Sketch of Los Angeles County, 17
Historical Society of Southern California, 63, 65
Hodge, Frederick Webb, 61, 77
Holder, Charles Frederick, 81
Home for All, 39
Hubbard, Elbert, 91
Hubbell, Stephen C., 33
Huggins, Julia, 125
Hunt, Myron, 97, 99
Hunt, Richard, 73
Hunt, Sumner, 49, 71

Isleta Pueblo, 49, 57, 61

James, George Wharton, 77, 87

Judson, William Lees, 85, 99
Judson Studios, 87

Keith, William, 53, 111
Kimball, Ward, 31
King, Duane H., 75
Knudsen, Valley, 35, 37
Knudsen (Tom and Valley) Foundation, 35
Kramer, George W., 43
Kysor, Ezra F., 15, 33

La Casita del Arroyo, 99, 101
La Miniatura, 97, 99
Land of Sunshine, 47, 67, 87, 89, 91
Landmarks Club, 47, 49, 57, 71, 89, 107
Lange, Emil, 119
Les Dames of Los Angeles, 35
Lincoln Avenue Methodist Church, 43, 45
"Lion's Den," 57
Little Corner of Local Art, 89
Longfellow, Gilbert, 39
Longfellow-Hastings Octagon House, 39
Los Angeles Beautiful, 37
Los Angeles Cultural Heritage Board, 27
Los Angeles in the Sunny Seventies, 13, 17
Los Angeles Star, 13, 15
Los Angeles Times, 23, 41, 43, 47
Lummis, Amado, 55
Lummis, Charles Fletcher, 23, 25, 47-65, 67, 69, 71, 77, 83, 87, 89, 107, 117
Lummis, Eve, 55
Lummis, Turbesé, 55
Lummis Home, 23, 47-65
Lummis Home Water-Conserving Garden, 63, 65
Lungren, Fernand, 59

Mad March Hares, 59
Makinson, Randell L., 117, 119
Mannheim, Jean, 95
Marston, Sylvanus, 105
Maxwell, Lucile, 53
Millard, Alice, 97, 99
Montgomery, Bishop George, 53

INDEX

Morgan, George Washington, 35
Morris, William, 85, 87, 91, 99
Mount Pleasant House, 17, 31, 33
Munk, Joseph Amasa, 75, 77

Nadeau Hotel, 21
National Historic Landmark, 97
National Register of Historic Places, 33, 35, 37, 39, 95, 97, 113
Newmark, Harris, 25
Nordhoff, Charles, 19

Occidental College, 25, 85, 91, 93
O'Melveny, Henry W., 69
Otis, Harrison Gray, 23
Our Lady of the Angels, 15

Paloheimo, Leonora Curtin, 111
Paloheimo, Y. A., 111, 113
Palms Depot, 29, 31
Pasadena Garden Club, 99, 101
Pasadena Historical Museum, 97, 103-113
Pasadena Historical Society, 113
Paul, Tim, 73
Percival, Olive, 89, 91, 99
Perry, Robert C., 65
Perry, William H., 17, 31, 33
Perry (William H.) Residence, 17, 31
Pico, Pío, 15
Pico House, 15
Pizarro, Francisco, 55
Poole, Caroline Boeing, 73
Powell, Lawrence Clark, 27, 93
Procter & Gamble Co., 117

Raymond Hotel, 111, 117
Ritchie, Ward, 93
Roehrig, Frederick, 113
Roosevelt, Theodore, 83
Rose, L. J., 41
Rose Bowl, 99
Roycroft Press, 91

Russell, Charles, 61

St. Vibiana's Cathedral, 15
Salvator, Ludwig, 17, 31
Santa Fe Railroad, 23, 51
Saunders, Charles Francis, 93
Semi-Tropical California, 19
Sequoya League, 49
Shaw, Richard E., 35, 37
Simmons, Frederick L., 45
Simmons, George A., 45
Simmons, Sidney M., 45
Sixty Years in Southern California, 25
Smaus, Robert, 43
Southern Pacific Railroad, 13, 23, 31
Southwest Museum, 23, 49, 51, 53, 57, 63, 67-79, 109, 111
Southwest Society, 67, 69
State Normal School, 25
Stearns, Abel, 21
Stetson, Charles Walter, 55
Stickley, Gustav, 85, 87, 93, 125
Strobridge, Idah Meacham, 87, 89

Temple B'nai Brith, 15
Throop Polytechnic Institute, 93, 95, 97
Truman, Ben C., 19, 21

University of Southern California, 21, 25, 85, 127

Valley Knudsen Garden Residence, 35, 37
van Eyck, Jan, 87

Wachtel, Elmer, 89
Wachtel, Marion, 89
Warner, J. J., 17, 27
Widney, J. P., 17
Williams, Dr. Herbert F., 41
Wright, Frank Lloyd, 97, 99